COMPANY TOWN:

An Oral History about Life in

Silver Bay, Minnesota, 1950s – 1980s

Published in the United States by:
Kent Kaiser, Ph.D.,
Project Manager & Editor

William M. Kelley High School
Silver Bay, Minnesota
Sponsor

This project has been made possible in part by the Arts and Cultural Heritage Fund through the vote of Minnesotans on November 4, 2008. Administered by the Minnesota Historical Society.

ISBN-978-1-60013-920-8

10   9   8   7   6   5   4   3   2   1

TABLE OF CONTENTS

FOREWORD

By Kent Kaiser, Ph.D., project manager and editor

As we gathered at the Silver Bay Country Club in May 2010 to celebrate our nephew's graduation from our own alma mater, William M. Kelley High School, my brother, Ward, and I were sitting with our dad, Chuck Kaiser, and our former principal, George Starkovich. As had happened many times before, our dad and George regaled us with stories about what it was like to live in Silver Bay in the "old days"—that is, from the 1950s, when the city was built to support the newly established taconite-processing operations at Reserve Mining Company, until the 1980s, when we had been in high school. At some point, Ward and I looked at each other and declared, "Someone has got to get these stories down!"

The more I thought about it, the more compelling the idea of recording Silver Bay's oral histories became—for a few reasons. First, Silver Bay's former status as a "company town," from the 1950s through the early 1980s, set it apart from most other small towns across America. Second, many people involved in the establishment of the plant and the city were still living. Still, many of Silver Bay's original settlers had died, thus making it more urgent to record the remaining people's stories.

Over the next few months, I thought more about how this oral history preservation project might proceed. I investigated the possibility of conducting the project under the auspices of William M. Kelley High School, with a grant from Minnesota's Arts and Cultural Heritage Fund administered by the Minnesota Historical Society. With a grant secured shortly thereafter, three Kelley High School students and I conducted an ambitious series of interviews with longtime and former residents of Silver Bay. We recorded these interviews and had them transcribed, which produced a couple hundred pages of raw transcripts. In addition, the Bay Area Historical Society, which had much earlier conducted and transcribed several similar interviews of Silver Bay residents (some of whom were deceased by the commencement of this project), made its archive available to us. By June 2011, we had a few hundred pages of interview transcripts. With a second Minnesota Arts and Cultural Heritage Fund grant received in fall 2011, we were able to organize, edit, and publish the interviews that are presented in this book.

Interviews with over 60 people have been compiled in this volume. Some people were interviewed individually, and others were interviewed in small groups. For the sake of readability, all the interviews have been deconstructed into constituent parts, arranged under seven broad topics, and cobbled together to simulate one cohesive conversation. Rather than presenting a typical history focusing on places, names, and dates, this project is meant to convey, from a more sociological perspective, a sense of what life was like in an iron mining "company town" in late twentieth-century America.

Working on this project on behalf of William M. Kelley High School, in support of preserving the oral histories of Silver Bay residents and the greater sociological phenomenon they comprise, was a complete privilege.

ACKNOWLEDGMENTS

This project has been made possible in part by the Arts and Cultural Heritage Fund through the vote of Minnesotans in the general election on November 4, 2008, to approve a constitutional amendment in support of protecting the state's natural resources and preserving the state's arts and cultural heritage. The fund is administered by the Minnesota Historical Society.

As the authorized officer for the grant, Joe Nicklay, principal of William M. Kelley High School in Silver Bay, Minnesota, provided administrative support for the project from start to finish. Kelley High School students Alexis Jacobson, Sabrina Jacobson, and Brett Mensing assisted during interview recording sessions. Alexis Jacobson also provided cover photographs.

Carefree Living of Silver Bay, under the management of Susan Spies, provided meeting space and refreshments for interview sessions.

Ruth Koepke of the Bay Area Historical Society opened the organization's archives as a source of interview transcripts. Excerpts of the organization's transcripts are marked with asterisks throughout this book.

Cody Durkee, Kelsey Ericson, and Lauryn White of Northwestern College provided transcription and editing services.

Interviewees:

Jim Andrews	Karl Jevning	Bob Oslund
Matt Banovetz	Delores Johnson	Arlene Pellett
Donna Beaupre	Irene Johnson	Ken Pellett
Tim Bjella	Wayne Johnson	George Pope
Karen Bock	Willis Johnson	Dave Prestidge
Ernest Bowman	Marjorie Jorgenson	Anne Przybilla
Evie Buetow	Chuck Kaiser	Art Przybilla
Harry Buetow	Judy Kaiser	Karen Rautio
Mary Carlson	Bob Kind	Helen Robinson
Bob Eckstrom	Dick King	Malvin Robinson
Ruby Eckstrom	Maggie King	Carol Roeben
Rose Elam	Ruth Koepke	Clarence Roeben
Marie Frey	Tom Langley	Lorraine Rustari
Jim Gordon	Pat LeBlanc	Walter Skalsky
Pat Gordon	Tootie LeBlanc	Mary Stahovic
Charles Heinzen	Mickey Lorntson	George Starkovich
Jenny Heinzen	Pat Lorntson	Evelyn Turonie
Harry Holmer	Lucy Malmo	John Turonie
Lloyd Houle	Tom Malmo	John Viola
Ed Hynes	Nancy Mismash	Marge Walentiny
Lois Hynes	Betty Oslund	Vern Walentiny
Fran Jevning		

CHAPTER 1

CONSTRUCTION

Dr. E.W. Davis of the University of Minnesota spent his career developing processes to convert taconite into a marketable product, iron pellets. By the 1940s, after some pilot testing, some steel companies were convinced that taconite could, in fact, be converted profitably into iron pellets. Reserve Mining Company, owned by Armco Steel and Republic Steel, decided to construct a processing plant in the location of what is now the city of Silver Bay, using taconite mined near Babbitt. The company bought property in both places—quietly, to avoid driving up land prices—and started surveying the areas. In the early 1950s, Reserve began carving into the wilderness both the industrial and residential facilities needed to support its operations. Ultimately, it would be necessary for hundreds of people to move into the area. Many members of the executive and managerial class of workers migrated to Silver Bay from Republic's operations in upstate New York and Armco's operations in Kentucky. Many of the workers on the floor came from rural areas of Minnesota and Wisconsin, where it was becoming difficult to make a living in the modernizing, streamlined, post-World War II farm economy.

Jenny Heinzen [later, Hanson]*: My maiden name was Betzler. I was born in 1936. I guess one thing I feel different than a lot of Silver Bay people is that I have never lived any place else. Everybody else is from some place. I have lived in Beaver Bay, Silver Bay, and Finland. Joe Betzler was my father, and he was also born in Beaver Bay. My great-grandparents came here in 1856. If you know in the golf course where the old Betzler cemetery is—across the river from the country club buildings—over there is where my grandparents' home was. It was so they could get water. She carried water from the river to do the washing. Our house was just about where the country club building is now. My mother used to call it "catch as catch can," because you did what you had to do. Sometimes [my father] might work for the town on the roads or something like that, sold stuff off the farm—milk and eggs and whatever—and they did a little logging.

We stayed at the farm until a representative of Reserve bought the farm. Our farm was one of the first pieces of land sold. It was many, many acres, because it went back a couple of generations. At the time my dad sold the farm, we didn't even know what was going to be happening. A lawyer by the name of Johnson, and it wasn't Wayne Johnson, was buying up land, and Beaver Bay people were speculating that maybe they were going to use that land for an airport or—they had all kinds of ideas. I guess some of the largest landowners were the first ones they bought from. They wisely bought from the largest landowners first. Then, they started buying down along the Shore when they got the largest pieces inland. Then we started hearing—it would trickle in—and finally we knew. When we moved from the farm, we moved onto Reserve land, and that's where we had the Silver Bay store. Reserve had already bought that, or what was to be Reserve, had already bought that, but they gave my dad a job as kind of caretaker of their land while construction was starting to take place. So, we ran the little store [Oscar Peterson's], where the silos at the plant are now, and my dad oversaw the rental of houses.

The first thing they did when we moved there was move the highway up. The road was down along the shore.

Jim Andrews*: Originally, Highway 61 went right through what is now the middle of the concentrator building. They were just moving it up to between what is now the crusher and concentrator [at the plant]. And just about the east end, a little further up the east end of the concentrator, Joe Betzler had a little grocery store, meat market, kind of a catch-all store in there.

Jenny Heinzen*: After they started to move the highway up—I remember the day—my dad came in from the outside. He'd been looking at a map on the fender of somebody's car and came in and said, "They're going to build the town site over the hill there in that valley." And, of course, all we knew of this valley was that John M. Jacobson had a hunting shack back in here and it was good blueberry picking. It was absolutely all woods. There was nothing here but a hunting shack and some places to pick blueberries. It was good deer country. So, it was kind of fun to watch the town get built. I wonder how many people have watched a town pop out of the woods.

Karen [Betzler] Rautio: We lived there for about six or seven years before construction really got going. We would hear a knock on the door at five, six o'clock in the morning, and somebody would say, "We're going to blast now. You have to get out." So, in our pajamas, we'd all pile in the car and drive a mile up the road and turn around and sit and watch. And there were rocks that hit the roof of our store. Once I was lying down at the lake, and there were rocks falling in the lake, zinging right over my head. We moved from there to Beaver Bay then.

Jenny Heinzen*: It was a different way of growing up from being on a farm to all of a sudden being in a store and meeting all these new people from all over the country, these construction people. Some were afraid [the plant] would change things too much. Others were grateful there would be jobs so they wouldn't have to leave the area. It was pretty mixed.

Pat Lorntson: It was one of those things where the people in the area had heard that this was coming for so long that they had just gotten to the point where they said, "We'll believe it when we see it." There was hearsay and all of that.

[My husband] Mickey went and surveyed the line. He said, "You know, we surveyed all the way from Babbitt down to Silver Bay." You know, it started out up there. That was in November of 1946, and most of these fellows were just out of the service—Mickey was, and so many of the other ones. And there was a McGraw Construction Company that hired some locals to work on the survey of a railroad. It lasted until April of 1947, and a grade was surveyed from just south of Babbitt to a location three miles northeast of Beaver Bay. That was kind of the beginning.

They walked the whole way from Babbitt to Beaver Bay. What they did was they started out in Ely and with snowshoes, it was winter—like 30 below. At the end of their workday, they would go back to Ely and stay overnight. As they progressed down the line, they would stay at places that maybe were summer resorts that were closed in the winter. They were walking in snow that was hip deep. But they were just glad for the work. They were just all in the service, and I think they were kind of anxious to be in on something at the beginning.

People were beginning to think that maybe something was really going to happen. Now that was in '46. Nothing else happened then until September of '51, when a company called Hunkin Arundel Dixon came to Beaver Bay and started clearing a plant site and a railroad grade to Babbitt, and the rest is history. So it was from '46 when they first were surveying until '51. Hunkin was here for quite awhile, and they did most of the work on this, making it into a town site.

So, Hunkin Arundel Dixon came in 1951, and in 1952 Mickey worked for a little while at DM&IR [Duluth Missabe, and Iron Range Railway], down in the ore docks. In the wintertime when they were steaming the ore, they needed people. Hunkin Arundel Dixon was here from '52 until '55 when Reserve Mining Company actually opened. You had to go and have a physical in order to be able to go to work at the plant. All these local people were really looking forward to a job, but when they went for their physicals, the doctor from New York that was here giving the physicals had so many people to choose from that he could pick and choose. My husband had passed his physical and had been at work for Reserve about two days, probably about two days, and then his brother was going to go and have a physical. The doctor told him, "Well you're in the beginning stages of rheumatic fever," and he never did go to work there. My husband's mother got to work there. His older sister got to work there. His youngest sister's husband was rejected because he was diabetic. His brother didn't go to work. It made uncomfortableness among that group of older people that thought, "Here we're gonna have a job," and everything. I think there was always that tension there, you know? The ones that didn't get chosen felt really left out, because then they had to go and find whatever kind of work they could. There really wasn't anything much for those people, just as it had been before.

There were so many people that came here looking for work, and that doctor was doing physicals all day long, and it was his say: "I can choose this one, this one, and this one." He could just pick and choose and we had heard he was getting so many dollars a person that he actually looked at so, you know, he could pick one out of ten. I know my brother had been in the service—in the Army for four years—and he came here and went down for a physical, and the doctor said to him, "Well you have something wrong with you, but it can't be fixed. He immediately went back into the Army, and they said, "Well we don't see anything wrong with you, except you have a big mouth." So a lot of people weren't any better off than they had been before.

Jim Andrews*: [My wife] Ginny and I were living in Minneapolis and had the two children then, and we simply didn't like the lifestyle we and the children were being exposed to. We decided to get out of there and the opportunity came, so I took it. Everyone thought we'd lost our minds—there was no Silver Bay at that time. The nearest town was Beaver Bay. January 1952, I came up here as a representative of the then State Employment Service. I came up here as a sub-office working under the direction of the manager of the Duluth office. I worked the employment, unemployment, recruiting, interviewing, and hiring for both the contractor and Reserve Mining Company.

It was a fun job. I worked with them for a year, and then came a major cut in state funds, and a whole lot of state jobs were eliminated. At that point, the contractor, Hunkin Arundel Dixon, commonly known as H.A.D., offered me the job as their employment manager, and I took it. I had that job, pretty much the same job, except I wasn't involved with the unemployment, until fall of 1954, when the contractor was almost winding up and Reserve Mining was then planning their big recruiting to fill the jobs they would need for their start-up. They offered me the opportunity to come with them, and again it was pretty much the same job, except it was specifically for Reserve Mining Company as opposed to the Hunkin Arundel Dixon.

I was in the employment office. The last many years, I was the supervisor of the office, and it included the seeking, recruiting, interviewing, testing, and hiring the employees for Reserve Mining Company, Silver Bay Division. In addition to that, my office handled the wage roll workers insurance plan administration, the Workers Compensation plan. We got involved in some testing, some training, some safety. We were kind of a catch-all for any of the employee and personnel relations types of activities involved with a mining company and employees as well as the local residents and visitors and guests. Our office was the access to the entire organization, so we wore a whole lot of different hats at different times.

My first office was a little white house that occupied the site that is now oil storage barrels just off the highway. The second office was what we now call the Boy Scout house, and that was down near where Bayside Park is now. Then we moved up to the building that is now the office building for the mining company.

We interviewed thousands of people over the time. In November, early December 1954, word came out that Reserve Mining Company was going to hire five to ten thousand people. Well, that was a bad time for the economy of both upper Wisconsin and here in Minnesota. That was when we were in the brown house, the old Boy Scout house. There were days when we had County Deputies, State Patrol, because there were cars lined up on both sides of the highway back to what is now East Beaver Bay Sport Shop. We worked from seven in the morning until sometimes ten o'clock at night. Our wives would bring us lunch and dinner down to the office. It was a busy, busy time, but it was fun.

At that time, we needed trades, we needed crafts, we needed semi-skilled operators—that is equipment operators—we needed technical people, we needed professional people and, of course, we had to have beginners, too—people who worked as laborers. We tried to select those we felt had the potential to move up into the company, because they were going to have to move. They would either move up or out.

Pat Lorntson: Accommodations were really poor when people came. There were a lot of people that had homes along the lake where the plant was, or where it came. They called it the chicken farm for some reason. So they took all these houses that were along the lake, and they moved them over, and they put them all in that area. There's three of them in a row over in Beaver Bay up above the apartment building that you can see from the highway. So they moved three of them up there. Oh, and I think they moved the fourth one up there, too. There was a lot of lifting of buildings and moving around, because they wanted that land free of houses. I think every cabin had people in it. It was not easy. They had down in the trailer court one building that was where you could go and get your laundry done, and then there was a grocery store. The first grocery store was a garage. Otherwise, there had been a grocery store in east Beaver Bay—Mattsons had a grocery store there.

Ruth Koepke: I came here as a Prestidge, and I came here in 1951 and watched the plant be built and watched it go down and watched it come back up again, worked there a couple times. My husband George Rosenau cut the first tree out in spring of '52, which is now Outer Drive, so I've watched the town since then, watched them move everything away from where the plant is, and my sister rented one of those houses that they moved. They were not winterized, they were summer cabins. They built a trailer court then that fall, and she moved into one of those cabins, and it's a good thing that the heat and electricity was furnished, because the wind blew the curtains about a foot away from the window. She paid $12.50 a month for a furnished cabin with heat and electricity.

Evelyn Turonie: I remember there was an old white house on the highway that has a big porch. I think it's still there. And that's where [my husband] had to sleep. That was the only place. There were other men sleeping there, and he had to pack up his stuff—his clothes and bedding and everything—everyday and put it in his car when he went to work.

John Turonie: Otherwise it'd be gone.

Evelyn Turonie: Because it would disappear.

John Turonie: [The company] started building the barracks in May of '52. I got in the barracks about fall of '52.

Evie Buetow: A lot of people lived at the trailer court during construction.

John Turonie: When we were doing construction work, we used to take our water cans and take the water right out of the lake—straight out of the lake.

Mary Carlson*: The construction people kind of paved the hardest part of it. When you think about it, this was carved right out of the wilderness. There was nothing here. So, the construction people cut a pretty good hole in the hill.

Fran Jevning*: I came in 1955 because my dad was a journeyman electrician [for Hatfield Electric] and his union sent him to work on the plant. He came by the office where I worked as a secretary and asked if I wanted to come along with them, and I did. I thought it would be a fun place to be, something different, and I'd maybe be here three or four months and work a little while. In the meantime, I met Karl, we fell in love and got married, so that kind of ended that.

Karl Jevning*: I had just gotten out of four years in the service, and I met one of my buddies back home as I was coming from Minneapolis and my discharge, and he was coming up to Two Harbors to steam ore. He wondered if I wanted to come along. He said it wouldn't last very long—a couple of weeks to a month and it's all done. I thought that would be something different. I'd never been up on the Iron Range, so I came along, we applied to steam ore, and we got on right away. It was DM&IR, the railroad company. We were steaming railroad cars. When they came from the Range, the red ore in the cold weather would freeze in the cars, and it wouldn't empty out, so we'd have to steam, with steam pipes, and heat that ore up for dumping. We worked for a period of days, and it got so hot, and it got so warm, we discontinued our steaming. We decided to take a trip up the North Shore, and the employment office was this side of East Beaver Bay. My buddy wanted a job for the winter. I was going to re-enlist again in the service, so I wasn't much interested, but we stopped and put in applications and got a call back for our physical. After we had our physicals, we could have gone right back. This was in November. We said no, we had obligations to finish steaming ore, and we'd let them know when our job was completed. I started working for Reserve on November 21 in '55. (We were done steaming by that time.) We didn't go back home; we went directly here and started working. I'm the only one that—there were three of us—I'm the only one that stayed.

There were houses on Davis converted for single guys. It was mainly construction people. We had a room there. We stayed there for an extended period of time. I would say six—maybe eight—people stayed in there. Just men. They didn't want you to have food. There were no refrigerators, but people still had stuff stuck in the windows to keep cool to make sandwiches for work and stuff. We ate in restaurants, mostly.

Jenny Heinzen*: I worked during construction years—I was a teenager—I worked at Berryman's Café and the Trading Post at Beaver Bay (Berryman's Café was what is now the Beaver Bay Inn). They had a tavern, general merchandise, a gas pump, and eventually a barber shop and grocery store in there. I worked for both of those, so I met a lot of construction people there. Lots of different kinds of people; some characters. [My husband] Chuck came up here fresh out of the army, and I met him while waiting on him. He was a "powder man" [dynamite technician] when we met.

We got married in December of 1953 in Two Harbors and came home and had a reception at my folks' house. There weren't any churches around here. Silver Bay wasn't here in '53. Previous to that, if we went to church, it was because a visiting minister was at the schoolhouse that Sunday. I think maybe the Ladies' Aid—there were a couple Ladies' Aid groups—primarily I think the Lutheran Ladies' Aids that would try and get ministers. I think there was a couple that came through different summers. We always had at least a week of summer Bible school, and that was from most any denomination.

[I went to school in] Beaver Bay, where the Green Door is now. I got most of my education there. We had eight grades there and then high school in Two Harbors. I went to eighth grade in Two Harbors, too, because the school was growing and they kicked the eighth graders out of there. I used to go [on the bus] about five minutes to seven in the morning and get home about a quarter after five at night.

Pat Lorntson: When they went down to the high school for ninth grade, it was a terrible time for these kids that went down there. I've heard so many stories after I got older. They either could ride the bus everyday, [or] they would work for their room and board down there. And I heard from girls that stayed down there and worked for their room and board how they were treated. And I just couldn't believe that that's how it was.

My husband got into a ninth grade mechanical arts class, or whatever they call it. They were supposed to draw something that they could build, and he drew a Christmas tree holder. He said that teacher stood over his shoulder and just berated him up one side and down the other, "You are so stupid. That's the only thing you can draw." He went on and on and on, and that was horrid. He dropped out in his junior year of high school because he said, "I'm a good truck driver, I know I can earn money, and I don't have to have this piled on me." We just heard so many things, and I felt so sorry. It was really, really, a hard time. I just couldn't believe that teachers and principals could act like that to a whole group of kids that just wanted to go to school. It was sad. That's still in the back of their heads. They can still remember that.

Karen Rautio: I started out going to school in the Green Door. When I was in the sixth grade, we started going to school in the houses at the end of Banks Boulevard. There was a first grade house, then there was a fifth and sixth grade house together, and then a second grade house. To start out with, we had no running water, so there was a little building on the hill up behind these three houses where we had to go. Our drinking water came in five-gallon cans. When it started running low, we got to go stand out by the muddy street and wait for a construction truck to come and pick that up and drop it off on his way back. It was quite an adventure. I went to school in Two Harbors for seventh and eighth grade then came back here and went back in houses again for ninth and tenth.

I still am a very shy, quiet person, believe it or not. They put me in a class [in Two Harbors] with nobody else that I knew. There wasn't a single soul in that class that I knew, and I was terrified. After going to school in a one- and two-room school and then a house, it scared the heck out of me. The teachers were great. They were very, very good. Some of the kids were really nice, and some were snobs. I can remember one of the first days. I had no idea where the cafeteria was—nobody bothered to tell us these things. I was sitting on a stairway crying when some kindly senior girl came and asked me what was wrong, and I told her, and she took me downstairs to the cafeteria.

Donna Beaupre: We always thought Two Harbors thought they were better than us.

Karen Rautio: One thing I remember about Two Harbors, when I was going to school there: Silver Bay got dial telephones. Two Harbors didn't have them yet, and I can remember walking down the hall one day and keep hearing somebody say, "Well, Silver Bay got dial telephones, and we don't have them." It was just, oh, such a terrible thing for those poor people not to have something that we had. Give me a break.

Donna Beaupre: But Two Harbors had the railroad, why would they whine about us having Reserve? Certainly the railroad must've helped them, I would think.

Evelyn Turonie: We had to go to Beaver Bay to get our mail. We had a post office box in Beaver Bay when we first came. Most women didn't drive, so I had three or four people, every day I'd pick them up and we'd go down to Beaver Bay and get our mail.

One day we went to Two Harbors, and we met this lady from the store in Beaver Bay [Mattson's, who] cashed checks for the men when they came out on payday. She had a shopping bag, and we gave her a ride home, and that was fine. We were going to go somewhere for coffee, and this lady said, "I'll take my bag with me." And she did. Nothing was thought about it, but afterward, when we came back out, got in the car and started home, I was sitting in the back seat with her, and she said, "Would you like to see what's in my shopping bag?" She opened it up, and it was full of cash. Because the next day they cashed the checks. That shopping bag was just a black plastic shopping bag, and it was full of money.

Marge Walentiny: In Two Harbors the people were not very nice about us being there. One time when we went there we stopped at the VFW for a drink, and we told the waitress how nice it was we were moving up to Beaver Bay, as they called [Silver Bay] then. So these two waitresses got in a booth right behind us. "These people that are coming to Beaver Bay, they're taking away all our jobs." They were so angry, and here I thought small towns were friendly. Well that one wasn't.

Two Harbors stayed open late on Wednesdays to accommodate us. So it was like a regular exodus [from Silver Bay], you know? We went down there, with all these cars going to the grocery store. That was a big deal. If you could get someone to watch your children, you could even stop at the VFW for a drink after. If you ran out of groceries of some kind and you couldn't get it at the store, it was fair game to borrow from someone. And then when you went to [Two Harbors], you had two lists, ones that you owed and ones that you bought.

Wayne Johnson: When the school district decided that they had enough schools, they abandoned [the Green Door]. Art Lorntson was the mayor, and I was the city attorney for Beaver Bay. So we went to the county attorney and asked, as long as the school district wasn't using it anymore, would they turn it over to the city? Well, he thought that was a good idea. We could get rid of the school and also do something for Beaver Bay to have a community building. He called the superintendent, and he asked, "What do you intend to use it for?" We said we wanted a community building. The superintendent agreed. A couple days later, they started moving the off-sales over to the Green Door. The superintendent found out about that, and a lady called and was just livid. She said, "Johnson, do you know that they're making a liquor store out of the schoolhouse?" Well of course the superintendent wanted to withdraw and get the title back, because he said he didn't want a liquor store in the schoolhouse. The reason it's called the Green Door, they had just painted the front door, put a new door on there, a sealed door, and it'd been painted green with a kind of vinyl coat that would hold on steel. They had a great big sign made—one of those big outdoor signs. The schoolhouse was painted red, with white trim, and the sign on it was "The Little Red Skol House." Of course the superintendent didn't like that. So as a compromise, we agreed to just take that sign down and call it the Green Door. And that name stuck.

Nancy Mismash: When we first came up, when Campton was the first school, the older kids went down to Two Harbors. It was one through nine here. The houses across the street were part of the school. There was an English house and a math house and a science house and a home ec house and all that sort of thing. So the kids would be just like at a college campus: They'd go across to the houses for their different classes.

George Starkovich: I entered seventh grade upon coming there to Silver Bay, and we went to school all grades K through eighth, maybe it was ninth. There wasn't enough room at Campton [the first school built] for everybody to go to school. They built the school called the Campton School. We had some classes like phy ed and music and shop class in the Campton School. The shop class was upstairs in what they call the projection booth, so you had to climb the stairs to get up to there. But the rest of the classes were across the street on Banks Boulevard. There was an art house, that's where you went to art class. Then there was a science house and a social studies house and an English house, and all of the core subjects were taught across the street. When you changed classes, you walked from one house to the next. At the appointed time the teacher would say, "Okay, it's time to go to class." There wasn't any big bell system, because they didn't have an intercom or anything. Everybody just knew what time to change classes.

You'd have to put your clothes on, if it was in the middle of the winter—you put on your parka or whatever—and you walked to your next class. That was always interesting and kind of a challenge, because as you walked along the sidewalk, you would be challenged by the seniority, that is to say you were supposed to step aside for the older kids to let them pass. That wasn't the school's rule; that was the kids' rule. Sometimes there was a little pushing and shoving as to who was going to get off the sidewalk and walk in a little bit of the snow. Sometimes an upperclassman—an eighth grader or ninth grader—would be going in the snow with the seventh grader, so it was an interesting thing.

Tom Langley: Yeah, I can attest to that. I was here during those days. I was in the class of '60. In between classes, especially in the wintertime, we'd walk from this house to that house, and that class would be coming this way. Of course, you'd always go, "Who's gonna get off the sidewalk? Well, we're not getting off." We had some great big burly guys in our class, and so did the class of '59. And we were coming down this way, Mr. Backlund was probably at the very end house or second to that, he was the math teacher. And we were coming down that way, and we cleaned their clocks, we knocked those guys off. We came to the door, and here's Mr. Backlund waiting for us at the door, and we thought, "Oh no." We got in, and he says, "Boys, get in and sit down." So we got in and sat down, waiting for the other shoe to fall, and he goes, "Nice going. You don't take anything from those older boys. You really cleaned their clocks." We thought we were going to be dead meat, but he was a pretty good guy.

George Starkovich: It was quite a melting pot, because we had kids from all over the nation because it was a new plant. There were construction kids—that means kids who were children of construction workers. There were plant kids, which meant that those were the kids who were sons and daughters or children of people that worked at the plant. Then there were children that lived in the surrounding areas who were children of parents who were employed in the logging industry. Some of them came from the Finland area, the Isabella area, and the Forest Center area. We had a big mix, and it was interesting because everybody had a certain identification. I was from Utah; somebody else might be from New York; and somebody else might be from Ohio; somebody else might be from Pittsburgh. So everybody was from all over the place, and you tried to brag up your area of the country.

Matt Banovetz*: I came back to Ely in 1951, after I graduated from the University of Connecticut with a degree in psychology. In looking for work, I was able to get a job as a laborer with McGraw Construction Company, who had a contract to refurbish the old pilot plant that had been built in Babbitt back in 1920, and worked as a laborer, including wagon drill operator, for $1.19 an hour. I was asked to go to work for Reserve as a part-time clerk. That job paid $1.50 an hour, so on August 27, 1951, I went to work for Reserve on a part-time job that ended about 35 years later. I worked as a time clerk, basically checking on construction workers that were on the property. We had to see that they were on the job twice a day, morning and afternoon. There were about 575 construction workers at that time.

As construction tapered down in 1952, I spent more time in the office, clerking and doing some minor accounting work. At that time, the head accountant, Galen Streimer, asked me if I would be willing to take some courses in accounting so that I would become more proficient. I wasn't too keen on that, so I asked some of the other people who were coming in from Armco and Republic—they would basically have the Reserve Mining Company responsibility—Armco basically had industrial relations and the pelletizing plant; Republic had the concentrator and crushing—as their people were brought in to operate those sections of the plant. I talked to Mike Tourje, who was the industrial engineer that Republic had sent up to be in charge of industrial engineering in Babbitt, and I asked if I could have a job working with him because I had a background in time and motion study. He said he would be glad to see that I got into his department. He recommended that I go down into the pelletizing plant and start at the bottom there and learn about pelletizing because that was something new in the industry and there weren't too many people—he thought it was the best opportunity for a young man. After a lot of soul searching—my wife and I discussed it considerably—in mid-August of 1952, I transferred down to the pelletizing department as a laborer, and from there, a man named John Begich and I were assigned the job of shoveling, with #2 shovels, the pellets that had been shipped from the pellet plant from Armco in Ashland, Kentucky. We had to shovel those pellets into a conveyer, which put it into an elevator, and that's how they charged the first furnace back in 1952. When it came time to start the furnace, I had been there long enough so that I was one of the four furnace operators selected. This was the top job in the pelletizer, and I had the good fortune of lighting the first furnace back in 1952.

I worked as a furnace operator for about a year, or a little more, and was asked to be a shift foreman, and so I took that job and fulfilled those requirements. We were basically changing—you see—there were four shaft furnaces and one of them was almost always down for remodeling, because we couldn't get the pellets that they wanted—either the tonnage or the quality that was going to be necessary, so we were in constant turmoil, but it was a great learning experience, because the operating people, when the furnace wasn't working, they worked as maintenance helpers, so we got to know a lot about the furnaces and the maintenance required while we were in the operating section. In 1954 they decided to try a new type of furnace that was the grate furnace, and that furnace was put on line around October of 1954. It became evident to most of us very shortly that we were able to make better pellets and could get out of trouble easier by operating that horizontal grate. In 1955—it was about January—it became time for the superintendents and assistant superintendents from the pilot plant at Babbitt to be transferred down to Silver Bay—we were going to supervise the final construction of the commercial plant down in Silver Bay.

In 1955—that was January—I was appointed superintendent of the pilot plant pellet division, in Babbitt, and I held that job until October of 1957 when the pilot plant was closed. The pilot plant—there were a couple of problems—they couldn't mine enough ore to keep both the pilot and the commercial plant going—that was one, but probably, more importantly, was the fact that with the small scale of operation we had in Babbitt could not compete with Silver Bay financially. However, we were making a superior pellet at the time in Babbitt, so we felt badly about that, but economics being what they were, they simply had to shut it down.

So in October of 1957, I was transferred out to the mine as the assistant superintendent to the mine. I went there with a great deal of apprehension, because I knew absolutely nothing about mining or mining equipment, and it was my good fortune to work with a general foreman named Steve Rebrovich. Steve took me under his wing and was a great help to me, teaching me about mining and mining equipment and, in fact, he and I used to go off by ourselves, get a piece of equipment, and he would show me how to check it out, start it up, and practice operating it. This is how I learned about mining equipment. Fortunately, in my years as superintendent of the pelletizing plant, I gained quite a bit of information, knowledge, and some expertise in labor management. For the most part, my job at the time was dealing with the people and union problems as well as learning about mining. It was a great learning experience, starting off very frightened, but becoming more confident.

George Starkovich: I was born and raised for the first 12 years of my life in Royal, Utah, which is a coal mining town. So I was used to what a company town was all about, because everything was centered around the company. I guess it was about 1952, I was moved from Utah to Babbitt so my dad could start working in the taconite industry in the pilot plant in Babbitt. We were up in Babbitt for the first couple of years. That was really interesting living up there, because we were some of the first people there, and we watched the town grow up around us. There were some big potato fields on one side of the town that had been purchased by Reserve. And that was kind of a staging area for all the houses. They were bringing the houses in on semis, and I can remember these dozens and dozens and dozens of houses just sitting there on blocking, waiting to be moved over to the town site where they were still preparing—literally a block away from the house in which we lived. We lived in one of the first houses that was constructed there. We saw these big earth movers actually constructing the town. It was interesting from the standpoint that we, as kids, were going to school, not in a school building but in other houses that had been modified from living spaces into spaces where kids could go to school. We had the elementary school kids going there to school in Babbitt in houses, and the upper grades were bused to Ely. We were there for two years, and then my dad was told he was going to Silver Bay.

So we moved into Silver Bay, and we moved up to Garden Drive, which had just been constructed. The lower end of town, Arthur Circle and Bell and Aiken and all those buildings were there. Campton School had recently been constructed, and as you proceeded up Banks Boulevard, the last street that was there in the old part of town was Davis Drive. We kids defined anything below Davis Drive as lower town and anything above Davis Drive as upper town. I started school up here in seventh grade.

The unique thing about moving in at that time was that anything past Davis Drive, the end of Davis Drive, right where Davis Drive meets Banks Boulevard, everything from that point forward was dirt. The streets were not completely laid out yet. The streets were there, but there was nothing except large rocks, probably about minus-four-inch size—the smallest rocks were the size of a baseball, maybe. That was the underpinning of the roads which were eventually going to be built, so all of the streets were laid out with those big rocks or gravel, I guess maybe it was.

John Turonie*: They had sharp crushed rock, and was that hard on tires!

George Starkovich: There were no curbs; there were no sidewalks. There was just clay, and the houses had been set on the foundations which had been poured, and the sidewalks were all wood—made out of just rough-cut one-by-sixes—so they were all boardwalks. They were something like pallets that you carry stuff on, but they were flat, so it'd be like two one-by-sixes running lengthwise and then all these other one-by-sixes about four feet wide laid on top. And they were laid end to end, and that's how people walked house to house or walked down the neighborhood. Each house where the driveways were, the boardwalk ended, and then there was a stone, like a stone driveway made out of smaller gravel. None of the driveways had been asphalted or anything, and none of the curbs were put in. There was no sod.

It's kind of exciting in a way to watch the town growing up around you, but I'm sure for the parents it was extremely frustrating because there was nothing but mud and dirt, you know, if it rained a little bit, there was no topsoil around the houses, it was all clay. So there was a joke, you know, if it rained and your kids went out to play, they'd go out to play and you'd retrieve them, and two days later you can go out and get their shoes or boots because they were still stuck in the mud. It was fun to watch the area grow up. And we lived on Garden Drive, and now Garden Drive was the last street in town at that time. We lived in 52 Garden, and I think 58 Garden was probably the last house on the street. Hays Circle, all the other circles—Lee and everything else, now we call that the "new section" of town—none of that was there, that was all woods and forests. The house that I currently live in on 24 Hays Circle, this was woods at the time. It was a neat time to grow up as a kid because you saw all this stuff happening.

Bob Linney, the president of Reserve Mining Company, or the first manager, was member of the 1948 or '50 Olympic bobsled team. So there were people from Fort Ticonderoga, up in that area of New York, and the New York people had, I wouldn't say kind of an "in," but they were part of the big plan, so to speak, because Reserve came from out east. Reserve was spawned by Armco and Republic Steel, so Armco and Republic were the parent companies. I think that the people from New York were designated as the people that were going to be the upper echelon or the management of the new facility.

Dick King: I went to high school [in Lyon Mountain, New York]. We lived in the country, but Lyon Mountain was a company town. The mine was very old. It might've gone back to the Civil War and really got going about 1870. That's when the railroad came. My dad was a foreman on the surface. I knew a lot of people there—some of those who came here.

Maggie King: Twenty-five families.

Dick King: Quite a few came here because they had the expertise that was needed. Some of the process was essentially the same magnetic separation. I worked there, and I managed to knock a loaded coal car off the tracks. I decided that it wasn't my forte. It was Republic Steel then. A lot of them came [to Silver Bay]. There were quite a few came from Kentucky.

Mickey Lorntson: They were all from the Armco group. The company was made out of two companies, Republic and Armco, and the ones you speak of from Kentucky were the Armco group. I think there were probably more from Armco, but I'm not sure. [The presidency at Reserve flipped back and forth between Armco and Republic.]

Maggie King: There were many people, I've met people whose beginnings, not from Ohio and not from New York State, that were from farms. Lots of people didn't have a future. They were helping hands on the farm; they weren't going to inherit the farm.

Matt Banovetz: People came here from all over. The mining company was very fortunate in 1951. It was certainly not a depression, but jobs were hard to find. Farmers were having a tough time, so when Reserve opened up, looking for people, they attracted people from all over the area, Minnesota and Wisconsin—people that were loggers, people that were farmers. I have a great deal of respect for these farmers. They were resourceful. They could figure out ways of doing things because they couldn't afford to hire somebody. They did it themselves. So Reserve ended up with a lot of good people, and that's what helped them really. I always thought that the hourly people contributed a great deal to the success of Reserve Mining Company, simply because of their background.

Tim Bjella: I was talking to a guy who came from Shelly, Minnesota, in the western part of the state. He was telling me he had worked for Reserve. He came here with, it sounded like, at least a half a dozen families. Whole groups of people from parts of the state would come together. They all knew each other.

Maggie King: They must've sent out scouts for hiring.

Mickey Lorntson: Like migration from Europe: Somebody came, and they wrote home and said, "Good, great opportunities. Come on over, you can get a job immediately, houses are only…"

Ken Pellett: Most everybody I would say, the biggest percentage anyhow, of people that worked for Reserve Mining Company in the early years were either from a farm or from a small town.

Tootie LeBlanc: Right. And very good work ethics.

Bob Oslund: We found out right away when we moved out of the apartments onto Hays Circle that there were all these highly skilled people around. There was a plumber living in the neighborhood, there was an electrician living in the neighborhood, there was a welder, there was an auto mechanic, so you just went to the neighbor to get help. Whatever it was, you'd go over and ask them, "I've got this problem." Whatever it was, they knew what it was and how to fix it.

The other thing that we later found out when one of my neighbors died: the medals that were written in the obituary. He had won the Silver Star, and nobody talked about that. And there were a number of men who had served in Europe and won medals—never talked about it. I know one individual I think started in Guadalcanal, went through the whole Pacific—never knew, he never said a word. But everybody else had that same experience. And some of them were drafted out of high school, never were able to finish because it would've been '44, '45, and if you were 18, you were gone [to war].

Ken Pellett: They weren't afraid to work.

Clarence Roeben: The people on the floor made the plant really what it is today. They put their ideas together, and they'd give it to the engineers, and they made something out of it. I realize a lot of boys didn't get a lot of credit for it, but in reality, them farm boys made that plant. They made it sing. They made it very productive.

CHAPTER 2

HOUSING

Reserve Mining Company had an immediate need for many employees in a sparsely populated area. Consequently, it was necessary for the company to orchestrate the construction of a city for its workers, rather than allow a city to emerge and grow organically over time, like normal. Employees involved in the plant's construction and early operations had to live in seasonal, tourist, and rental properties that existed in the area. In its earliest days, the company also built barracks for its workers, and eventually Reserve contracted with construction companies to build the houses in Silver Bay. Indeed, Reserve paid the cost of installing the complete city of Silver Bay, including not only houses but also utilities, landscaping, streets and gutters, sidewalks, and municipal and commercial buildings. Reserve sold the houses and commercial buildings to John W. Galbreath, real estate magnate and owner of the Pittsburgh Pirates baseball team, and thus his company controlled the housing market in Silver Bay. Only Reserve employees and others deemed essential to the support of Reserve's operations were allowed into the houses—and at first only in rental arrangements. Later, people were allowed to purchase the houses, on a prescriptive, hierarchical basis, with no down payment and ridiculously low mortgage payments and property taxes.

Matt Banovetz: Both Reserve Mining Company and Erie [Mining Company] had the problem of, "How are we going to get enough people close enough to make it worth their while to live and work here?" So both companies built towns. Hoyt Lakes got built by Erie, [Babbitt and Silver Bay by Reserve]. For whatever reason, the people living in the communities, to start with at least, depended on the company for almost everything. Anything that somebody needed or wanted, they would call the company. For the most part, the company cooperated.

John Turonie*: They would come in with a semi-truck with a house. I'd go to work and by the time I came home, there was a house there.

Ruth Koepke: They built two or three a day, or more than that, sometimes.

[Silver Bay] was built to be a model city, so it was terraced, and these houses were built with washers and dryers. Most of the workers came off the farm, and they'd never lived so good. When they started, they didn't want any clothesline poles, TV antennas, gas tanks. When people started tying line from their front porch to the electric pole, they decided they could put up clothesline, but it was supposed to be a model city with none of that stuff out.

Evelyn Turonie: We could not have a TV antenna; we could not have a clothesline. You couldn't have a TV antenna, but our buddy was a TV man and helped put it in the attic.

Anne Przybilla: The housing manager for Galbreath and told us there are no alleys in this city. This town has been set up perfectly, no alleys.

John Turonie*: They changed the rules later.

Lloyd Houle: We were concerned about getting television.

Marge Walentiny: [There was] this guy, he worked for the phone company, and behind his house were a bunch of trees. He put an antenna up in the tree and got it to work. When word got around, we started going there, even though we weren't invited—that didn't matter to us. Finally, the people got to the stage where they were rebelling. They wanted their TV, and that's all there was to it. And the company finally relented and said okay. So by then, you should've seen: It was just like Christmas trees going up with all the antennas.

Vern Walentiny: They wanted you to leave the house as you found it.

Marge Walentiny: Even the paint on the inside, no you could not touch those houses! You were lucky they let you bring in your own furniture—until we owned it. And that's when everything went. That's why I said the antennas just came up like someone waved a magic wand over 'em.

Vern was a carpenter, so he knocked down a wall in one of our houses so another lady would see that, she'd get her husband to knock down a wall in his house, or else somebody'd put a little sand by the door, you know, to make it look like a foyer (or whatever it's called), and pretty soon you'd see a bunch of those lined up like that, too, so a lot of people that didn't have imagination gleaned a lot of information from those that did.

We were lucky to get a cream-colored one. I think they felt sorry for us. We got the cream-colored one, and then they had kind of a light ishy green, and then a tan house. They had these tile floors. The tile was brown with a little bit of cream and a little bit of orange in them. And I hated it, I hated it with a passion, and so did everyone else who had it just like it. I'd try to polish it. You couldn't do anything with it. It looked like you'd never touched it. And then of course they'd say, "Oh you got a cream-colored house. Our house is tan." "What color is your...?" "Oh we got a green house; we like ours." Then we had our TV set that was just sitting there. We couldn't use it because we couldn't put an antenna up, so it was like a nice piece of furniture. I put a vase of flowers on top of it. That's all I could do with it.

Marie Frey*: We heard there was a lot of work here. We were up at Isabella and Murphy City when we first came. Walt worked for Erie Mining. Then he had a chance to get on with Galbreath. When we came here [in 1953], Walt actually did work for Galbreath. We couldn't buy a house right away. We had to rent. I can recall there were about six colors that all the houses were painted. One house was grey, one was fawn, one was cream etc. There were about five or six colors, but the whole house was painted one color, even inside. After we bought our homes, when we were allowed to buy them, boy, it was a great thrill to be able to paint each room a different color.

Marge Walentiny: We moved to Silver Bay in 1954, and we had a son who was two months old at the time. That was our oldest one. The reason we got a house right away was because they needed a medical, an X-ray technician, which is what Vern did. It was a two-bedroom house. We made friends right away because everyone was from out of town there because it was a brand new town and you got acquainted very early or else you were very lonely. We came from the big city of

Minneapolis, which I thought would be a culture contrast to me, but it wasn't that bad at all because we met all these people from bigger towns and they also had these various accents that we had, so it was like a melting pot.

There were people that had houses, and they saw someone else and liked it better and someone liked their house, then they would swap, with the blessing of the company.

Vern Walentiny: I think the charge was $75 for the paperwork, or something like that.

Marge Walentiny: However, there were a few that did not want to pay that money, so what they did was they switched on their own. So if you went knocking on the door, and you thought someone that you knew lived there, somebody else answered the door because they had already swapped houses with somebody else.

We found out that this couple couldn't afford theirs, so we went to the company and told them we would like to do this. They said okay, because we wanted a basement, and they said, "Alright, if you do this, we will waive the fees for you." So we got by on that.

The people we changed our houses with: We kept getting bulletins at our address from the church that they belonged to. We'd just take them over without correcting the address. Then this one day, the minister came knocking on our door, and he said that he was such and such a minister, and we said, "Well come in," you know? You did that to people. So he came in, and we visited for awhile, and he said, "Well I noticed you haven't been in our church for awhile." I said, "Well what church are you from?" And he said, "Sychar." And I said, "Well we go to the Catholic church." He said, "What?" And he said, "I'm all mixed up here." Another lady, a friend of ours was there, and she said, "Are you looking for…" whoever these people's name was. And he said, "Yeah, are you that…" I said, "No. We are the Walentinys. We switched houses." So he thanked us and apologized, and I said, "Don't apologize, it was very nice visiting with you." Then he went to call on the lady across the street about a week later. I had told her about this, and then he said, "Are you Mrs. Lompton?" She said, "Yes I am." "May I come in?" He wasn't taking any more chances.

Lucy Malmo: We were offered a house to live in at that time by Sychar church. There were three colors of your materials. They were either a tan or a gray or a cream color. So we chose the tan color, and it was repainted for us, so we did have a clean house to move into. That was in '55. We didn't have a garage. We didn't have a driveway. There were no sidewalks or anything yet. Then, in a couple years, they said, "You have to get out of your house." We were given six months to get out of our house. We were renting. I think it was about $75 a month or something. We had to move out for the company people.

We weren't allowed to buy a house. It was like the teachers. We couldn't buy a house in town. We had to move, so we had to pick a lot. I was about five months pregnant, and it was wintertime. Then there was an extra lot up on Hays, way down on the upper side. And we asked if we could buy the middle lot and split it with the neighbor so we each had a lot and a half so that we'd have a little more room.

Absolutely not: One lot, that's all we could have. So we built the house through the winter of '57, and that's a long story. We were supposed to move in on February and in July we moved in. The house wasn't done.

Tom Malmo: It didn't even have a front window in it.

Lucy Malmo: We didn't have a sink. The contractor had taken our money and finished another house with our money. We just moved into the bare, gray plastered walls, and that was in '58, so it was pretty miserable. I mean, we had a three year old, and the baby was born in March, and we had to move into this shell. I filled every nail hole in that house, and then we had to finish it, and that took a few years. We didn't have any money left to finish, of course. [Our daughter] Beth would come running home in her stocking feet. Her boots were stuck in the mud somewhere, so she'd have to take me back to where it was so I had to find where the boots were and get her all cleaned up. We didn't have a yard, of course, and so the swing set was across the street on the boulevard. So she had to run across the street to play on the swing set.

Evie Buetow*: I can interject here the story about the first person to welcome us to Silver Bay—it was 1954. Tom Malmo, who had the Malmo Drug store, said, "Welcome to Mud Flats," because, Silver Bay was nothing but a mess of mud, even in June. No sidewalks in that whole new section up on Banks Blvd where we lived. No grass, no sod, no nothing. Not even mud—clay. It was not nice.

Lucy Malmo: Sychar Church wasn't there, and I could see down from our house—we were on the corner of Edwards there, and I could see down to the shopping center [and our store]. I was eight months pregnant, and I was supposed to put a red shirt against the cream-colored door if Tom needed to come home, because we didn't have a telephone or anything.

George Starkovich: Teachers at the time could not own a home in town. The only place that they could live was in the apartment buildings that were located on Bell Circle. And they were allowed to live there in town, or they would have to make their own arrangements to live out of town somewhere. We had teachers that lived in Beaver Bay. Some lived in the trailer court, located where the cement plant is now, just east of where North Shore Oil and Petroleum is at the present time. There was a very large trailer court where a lot of the personnel and families from Hunkin Arundel Dixon lived.

Betty Oslund: When I came, there were four buildings of six units—apartment buildings—six units in a building. There were two of these units that were for single women who were working here. The one that I was in had three single women who worked at Reserve. When I came to teach in Silver Bay, I needed a place to live, and so they said there was an available spot in that unit. I lived there for a couple of years until I met Bob and got married. The interesting thing about that was, we couldn't buy a house, as other teachers couldn't. But it was either the year that I left or the next year that there were two teachers, single teachers, that were going to live in [the apartments]. When they came in August, right before they came, they found out they didn't have a place to live. The company had taken that unit, and they were giving it to somebody else—maybe a married family. So they had boxed up the things that they left there, and they had to scramble to find a place to live.

Lorraine Rustari*: For single people, life in Silver Bay during the latter part of the 1950s was not ideal. Single people were not allowed to buy homes, so I lived in the Bell Circle apartments after living in Two Harbors for two years. What prompted the move was the fact that I did not own a car or drive. I was dependent on car pools, most of which were driven by reckless young fellows. On Friday nights our driver would stop off at the Green Door and purchase a six-pack of beer. In order to consume the beer without getting caught, he would take the old Beaver Bay Road to Two Harbors. Beer cans were thrown out the window at random. After a few harrowing experiences, I decided to buy a car and learn to drive myself, so I moved to Silver Bay. The rent for the Bell Circle apartments for teachers and stenos was $31 a month with all utilities paid, except telephone. The apartment housed four people. The only stipulation was that you could not "choose" your roommates—any stranger who wanted to come in was allowed to rent. I was fortunate at that time, as my roommates were teachers. Ruth Williams, the home ec teacher, after many heated meetings with Galbreath and Reserve, persuaded them to allow single people to buy homes, which prompted me to buy a home in 1965.

Anne Przybilla: [After my husband, Art, was hired], Reserve Mining announced this big expansion and Denny Dalin, who was teaching here then and was a friend who had recommended Art, called and says, "You guys have got to get up here because housing is really going to be scarce." So we came up, that was like in April, but we didn't get up here until after school was out, and we ended up living in motel unit in Little Marais at Fenstads' Resort. My kitchen was a unit that had two burners and a sink, and a refrigerator underneath. We lived up there until November.

Art Przybilla: 16 by 16 feet. Three rooms in those 16 by 16 feet.

Anne Przybilla: Three rooms and a bath. And we [moved to] right at the base of the hill there up the road from the Beaver Bay Inn, I don't know what it's called now. And then we lived there for a year, and then finally an apartment became available, and by that time it was basically teachers that were living in all of the apartments.

Art Przybilla: We were told when we first went into Galbreath's to get housing—that's where we were told to go—and they told us right straight out, there were many too many people working for the company, you don't have any chance. It was truly company controlled, who would get housing.

Bob Eckstrom: I had to live in the barracks at first, and then about the second month, we rented a little trailer. That went alright for one month, and then they sold the trailer, so we didn't have a place to live. When I couldn't get a home, I told the superintendent, I maybe have to go. That night he came with a slip with 19 homes for me to look at. So there.

John Viola: When I came to Silver Bay, I wasn't able to buy, either.

Ken Pellett: I came to work for Reserve Mining Company in April of 1959, and at that time I was single, and I lived in the barracks or the dorms over there behind the main office. Originally when we came here, everybody who was single lived in what we called the staff dorm. It was two-story construction building over behind the main office, and we did have a big commissary there. We, 90 percent of us, ate our meals there, and it was kind of like an army barracks. Not to say there wasn't plenty of parties. It was a real good place to get started. First I lived in the barracks for a year or so, and then I bought a mobile home in Beaver Bay trailer court. After we got married, we started looking at homes. At that time you had to be an employee of the company or a salaried person to be able to buy a home.

Dick King: The first [trailer court] was right around the corner from Palisade Baptist. There was a row of tourist cabins. Right downhill from them was all these shiny, new aluminum trailers all lined up, and then, right in the middle there was a laundry for everybody.

Charles Heinzen*: We couldn't get a house in town. Everything was full. We were living in Finland. Sometime after, we moved into town. I started for Reserve in February and moved into a house in May. We bought a house at 18 Dodge Lane. It was only a few months.

Nancy Mismash: Well we came up and, because my husband worked for Reserve, we could get a house, but we could not get a house with a basement, because we didn't have any children. We had to have children in order to get a basement house.

Tim Bjella: We moved here in the fall of '58, and of course there were no homes available for non-Reserve workers. The apartment we had was 36B Bell Circle. They were very nice apartments. They had hot water heat, and the floors were nice and warm, it was very, very comfortable.

Maggie King: I came as a single. I lived in the apartments and was told that there were a few choices, and one was to live out of town. I could've rented a house, which actually I really would've liked, because I think the property went all the way down to the lake. The other was to live in the apartments with two teachers from Ely who commuted. They were three-bedroom apartments, and they were accommodating.

Anne Przybilla: When we lived in the apartments, we lived in the end of one building, and [my husband, who taught theatre,] came home after rehearsal one night and went in the wrong building and realized it after he was in. I heard these feet come thudding along the far side of our building, and he came in, and the door slammed.

Art Przybilla: I would never have known, except the cat didn't attack me. I went into the wrong house.

Anne Przybilla: He was so worried, because there was rumor of a window peeker around, and he said, "What if they think I'm the window peeker?"

Pat Gordon: We arrived in Silver Bay on February 12, 1970, and lived in the apartments on Bell Circle. They were quite warm in the winter as the floors were heated. The most memorable time living in the apartments was that the bedrooms were located on the second level. We had a great view of Lake Superior and watched as the ore carriers came and left Silver Bay. It was a beautiful sight. During the summer nights, our windows would be open and we could hear the train whistles, the train cars hooking up, and the taconite filling up the bins at the crusher.

George Pope: [We lived] at 34E Bell Circle. After a few years, somehow we were able to buy a home, and we'd never owned a home before.

Dick King: You had to be a Reserve employee to get a house. I remember when the school nurse was kicked out of her house that they had only rented to her. They'd had an opening, and nobody needed a house at that time, so they rented to Dorothy, and then [later] they told her she had to leave because they had a Reserve employee.

Judy Kaiser: We came here in 1966. And at that time, teachers were to live in apartments, and we had a difficult time, because the apartments were full. We started looking for a place to live, and Galbreath had permitted us to look at houses, and there were only two available. One was up on Chase Lane, and one was on Davis—both slab houses—and they permitted us to purchase the house on Davis, but at that time I think all the teachers I know lived in apartments.

Dick King: I was the first single person to be allowed to buy a house from Galbreath. They were opening up now; non-Reserve employees were getting houses. That was on Davis. Must've been about '63, '64.

Chuck Kaiser: When we got here, there were two houses in town that we could buy—that were for sale—and then we bought the one at 42 Davis. That was it for us, and we didn't have to find something out of town, but by that time, there was no rule saying we couldn't buy one—there just weren't any available. Galbreath wouldn't do anything for us, but they told us we had to go talk to the people that were selling them, which we did, and we bought one of them. We lived in a slab on Davis, and then we moved into one on Gibson that had a basement.

Ruth Koepke: The houses, like those that were built up there and Davis and Drake and all those: It was Harnischfeger out of California that built that group. They should've stayed in California, because they weren't used to snow. They all had those nice sunroofs, and in Minnesota, you get that much snow, you go out and shut the door. I always said Harnischfeger should stay in California, and you should get local contractors. I always called them "Little boxes, little boxes, and they all look just the same." My parents up on Burk one night heard a noise, and there was footprints, snowy footprints, they never locked the door, and someone had gotten in the wrong house. That was easy to do, because they all look looked the same.

Everybody's house had about four colors that they painted. They must've gotten a really good deal on paint. I said I would never have any beige in a house again, because every room was painted the same. They had fawn, the called it, and a pale yellow and a pale green, a gray. The floors all had either brown or black tile. If you wanted it to look nice, you had to wax it every week, and then you'd look down the hall, and it still didn't look too good. When we moved up on Hays Circle, every other house had pink cabinets or aqua. Here these were all white Republic Steel. Those were still Republic Steel in a steel town, but pink and aqua and peach. I always said, "A kitchen needs to have colors of either fruits or vegetables. I don't know too many that are pink." So I said, "Well, if it's going to be way out, I'll paint my walls purple." So I had pink and purple.

Tootie LeBlanc: Every house had brown tile in it.

Arlene Pellett: When it was first waxed, and after the chair scratched it, you know, it was horrible.

Pat LeBlanc: And every house had slate shingles. There was a single-car garage in every home. The slab homes had an extra-deep garage because most of them had an oil tank in back. And some had, instead of a washer and dryer, a deep freeze or something in the garage, and it worked out very well.

Ruth Koepke: As well as all looking alike, in Drake Circle, the doors didn't unlock went you went out, so if it went shut on you, then you'd be locked out. So we'd go to a neighbor until we found one whose key fit our door. On Drake Circle, we had probably three keys that fit all the houses.

John Turonie: I started here working for construction in '52. And it was all rock moving. It was hard to imagine that there was going to be a taconite plant here. But it worked out. In '54 the foreman said to me, "They've got a few houses built up on Burk Drive." He says, "You can have your wife come, and we'll give her a set of keys, a master key, to five houses she can pick from." "Yeah," she says, "What if I go into and somebody's living in it?" He says, "Well, if you go in there and somebody's living in there, you'll know it."

Chuck Kaiser: My wife and I came up for the first time to interview for the job. I already knew I had the job, but I still had to come up here. We drove into town, and of course there were hardly any trees that were over three feet high, and all these houses looked the same. And remember back in '66, there was a song, "Little houses on the hillside…

Maggie King: Yeah, "of ticky tacky."

Chuck Kaiser: That was running through my head as we came into town, and my wife said, "I will never live in one of those houses." And we spent the next 45 years living in one of those houses. That was just my first impression of this town. But all the houses weren't the same, because the corner houses were bigger, and they were not for the rank and file. There, people that got into those houses that other people couldn't. That was the first thing we found out about when we came here—it was kind of passed on to us. You look at it differently, because at first, everything looked the same, but then when we're told this, we used to, "Oh, that house is different, sits different, got a different outside…" And like I say, oh and the house across the street from us on the corner was like four feet bigger than the other houses were, and that was a slab. The corner houses were bigger, and they were for management.

Mickey Lorntson: Corner houses were the top.

George Starkovich: On every block, virtually every block, on the corner there is a larger home. Most of the homes were just typical pitch roof or regular. But the houses on the corners had an L shape to them, and those were designated for people who were assistant superintendents and such. They wanted them to be living in an area where the workers lived, but they also wanted them to have a little bit more prestige in terms of the size of the house that they had.

The upper echelon had the big homes down around Arthur Circle, and the other upper echelon folks and the superintendents of the various departments had the houses up on the hill. Dr. Davis, who invented the process had the house way at the top of the hill. He was the one who perfected the process for extricating the iron ore from taconite and processing it into pellets. He did that down at the University of Minnesota. Then you had people that were head of the various departments. There was a gentleman who was the chief financial officer of Reserve who lived up there. Another was the superintendent of the pelletizing operations. And the biggest house in town was the guest house, and it's the only house in town that had clay tile on the roof.

Mickey Lorntson: That was a quality house, that one.

Chuck Kaiser: It had a bowling alley in the basement.

George Starkovich: That was where people who were from out east, who would come to visit the plant and inspect the facilities, would stay. They would come in on the ore boats. They had people from town who would act as wait staff and housekeeper cleaners and maids and such that would take care of the facility and do the cooking and things of that sort. It was a pretty well-planned town, in terms of being in a company town.

Tim Bjella: There was a section of town called Snob Hill. Everybody knew who was up there. They were somebody.

Pat Lorntson: They were the bigwigs.

John Viola: The housing was separated. In other words, there was housing for staff, there was housing for foremen, and there was housing for the workers—the hourly workers—and you can find that in town now, if you look at some the houses. If you look down on the lower part of Arthur Circle, those people were all management staff people. If you go up on the cul-de-sac off of Edwards and Edison, those people up in there were all management people, primarily brought in here from New York. There were a lot of New York people there. They were familiar with making pellets because they had made pellets in New York before this plant was ever built. There were also some Armco people that came in. Armco brought them in here, and Armco had done some experimental work on pellets down in Middletown, [Ohio]. The other thing is up on the hill you'll see, the doctors in town. The doctors in town had their housing up there. There were two doctors, Doc Bloom and Doc Haase. And then they had the house that was built by the fellow that had developed the pellets down at the university. But they were separated, so there's certain sections of the town where management people and supervisors got to live. You talk about corner lots, if you notice that a lot of the corner lots had, or still have, a larger house than what's adjacent to them. They were separated out because there were going to be foremen in those houses, and that's how they had the distinction made. If you were a foreman, you had the orange hat, you got the preference for that house.

Matt Banovetz: You know, you had the group down around Hays, then you had another group up around the Arthur Circle, then up on top of the hill where Doc Davis lived. They didn't do it in Babbitt, but they did it in Silver Bay. In Babbitt there was a difference, although it was not restricted. There was three sizes of houses in Babbitt. They had a small house. They called it an A house. Then they had a C house and a D house, so that they had different size houses, but they were mixed around the town. When I moved to Silver Bay, it made me think that they made a big mistake, the way they laid out the town and built those houses—to segregate management, so to speak, in many respects. I don't know who made that decision— somebody did—because as I said, they didn't do it in Babbitt, but they did in Silver Bay. And I always thought it was bad, a bad situation.

Tim Bjella: I live up on Snob Hill. Mine and all those south of there were mining company houses, or Galbreath houses. As you went across the street, we had two doctors over there that built their own, and then Buetows [the dentist's family] and up to the top of the hill where Dr. Davis's house was. That was probably why they called it Snob Hill. But I never knew any of them that really were snobbish.

Maggie King: Buetows were there a long, long, long, long time.

Evie Buetow: When we first came to Silver Bay, they were looking for a dentist, and we had just come back from two years in Germany. My husband was working for my father who was dentist at the time, so we thought, we love the Northwoods and the canoe tripping, so we thought let's go take a look at what the housing is like. This was my first introduction to what a company town was going to be: Bob Wieger, the town manager, drove us all around town showing us all these slab houses, very small houses. I had said to my husband, "I don't know if I'm going to move, if we have to leave something that we're used to here from the Cities." So we went, he would say, "That's available. That's available." This is 1955, mud everywhere, there weren't even sidewalks and so forth. Every once in awhile we would drive by a larger house that was empty. "How about that one?" "No, that's a supervisor's house." Then we'd go another few blocks, and there's another empty larger one being finished. "How about that one?" "That's the foreman, supervisor," whatever. I said, "You mean, if I wrote you a check tomorrow for cash for that house," big joke, "that we couldn't have it?" He said, "No. That's just the way the town is built." I thought, "Oh brother, what are we getting into here?"

There was, the way the town was built, I would call it sort of a caste system at the time. We were sort of put into a unique position in a way because, when we moved into a house on Banks Boulevard, and Mr. Kelley was the president at the time, he came to Harry for a massive amount of dental work. He had this faith and trust in him and really liked Harry. So it started like a father-son relationship for awhile. Then came the time when we got notices we had to be out of our houses, the rental houses. Any teacher or business person or anyone not related to the plant had a date to be out of those rented houses, with either plans to build or plans to buy a house, probably not close to town. At the time, Mr. Kelley was so wonderful and said to Harry that there were two lots left up on Kent Lane. One was going to be chosen by the next man coming in to be treasurer or whatever, and whichever lot he didn't want, we could have—we'd pay for it. But he would put our name on the lot and let it be known at Reserve that Dr. Buetow could buy the lot and build a house. It was ours. That's how we got to build our house up there. That put us into the Snob Hill category.

Lloyd Houle: Our superintendent was Bill Grabel, and he lived up on Burk Drive to start with, and then he moved down on Bell Circle. Pretty soon they told him he was going to be superintendent, and he had to move. They all had to move. I remember we were looking for a larger house. We had three girls and a boy, and so we looked at the U.P. [United Protestant Church] parsonage. Matt Banovetz lived next door, and he says, "I'll tell you one thing, boy, if you come up here, you'll never have better neighbors." Pretty soon they moved out of there. Blanchard was another one. They had a guy named John Ott that was superintendent at the powerhouse, and he had some problems down there, and he got fired, and Blanchard, he got promoted. They told him he had to move. We laid out all the houses, the guest house and all the houses at the top of Snob Hill. They had whatever they wanted.

Mickey Lorntson: [Pat Bryant] went down to the log house after [her husband, Bill, the plant president] died.

Pat Lorntson: She was made to leave that house.

Mickey Lorntson: Yeah, she didn't qualify for that house after he died.

Maggie King: How do you like that? The president's wife.

Mickey Lorntson: Yeah, she didn't own it.

Pat Lorntson: I think they needed it for somebody else that was higher up. Yes, she was made to leave that house. And she cried.

Mickey Lorntson: Ed Schmidt took it over next.

Lois Hynes: When Bill Bryant was president, I was working in the employment office, and we had some problem with our yard. It ended right at the end of the garage, and I thought, "Come on now, we need some backyard here, not just this field and everything." So I went up and talked to Bill Bryant. And I said, you know, this would be kind of nice if they could fill in and give us a little more backyard. A few days later, they were up there plowing dirt and sod and giving us more. Well, Jim Andrews in the employment office, he almost had a stroke: "You went up and talked to Bill Bryant about your backyard?" I said, "Well, I didn't know where else to go, and he's the president, so start at the top and find out where to go." He was so pleasant about it. I just thanked him.

Evie Buetow: You just had to give him a chance.

Lois Hynes: They didn't know that we hadn't gotten the whole full area.

Ed Hynes: There's some huge big rocks out there they bulldozed all the way up and put a culvert under [the neighbor's] backyard. They never called back—they just did it, and we appreciated it.

Betty Oslund: We built our house around '61. That was built up on Hays Circle, and there happened to be a lot left there. Galbreath had a builder come in, and they had a choice of, I think, three or four house plans, so you chose one of those four, and there were four or five others that were built just like ours, a couple of them up on Nelson, and one over on Hays, and then ours. So for awhile then, they were trying to make houses available to people, and you could build them. They had a builder come in to do that.

Anne Przybilla: You only had the choice of these different ones. I know when we first came to town, one of the things I remember is you would be invited to someone's home, like a student's home for dinner or something like that, whoever went into a house, they'd look around and say, "Oh you did this to your house," because the houses were so much alike inside, and everybody was looking to make it a little different. One of the first things, people would look around and say, "Oh you did this. Oh you did that. Oh I would never have thought of doing that." That went on for years.

Marge Walentiny: When we came, they had all this red clay, and it would get on the shoes and boots and come in the house, if you had little children, they're not going to stop to take off their boots, so constantly mopping and getting it clean. No sooner clean than the kids'd go outside again and same thing would happen. So finally it got the point where it was just an untold thing: You went by the door, you took off your shoes. The ladies who were more modest would carry slippers. Some of us just went in our stocking feet, and this continued long after the grass was there and everything. It was so ingrained in us that it was kind of nice to sit there with no shoes on. So that's what we did.

John Turonie*: We had boardwalks for sidewalks.

Lois Hynes: Being a city girl from Minneapolis, I got quite a kick out of walking on the board sidewalks up in the shopping center.

Evelyn Turonie*: Every house had boardwalks. No streets at all, no curbs, no sidewalks, just those boardwalks.

Pat Lorntson: The kids would go out to play, and when it was time to come in, the mothers would go out and pick the kids up and take them out of their boots, because their feet were stuck in the ground. We had a lot of red clay in this countryside. But it was a mucky, muddy mess for a long time.

Marge Walentiny: People could hardly wait for the grass. It would be like God brought it in by himself it was so [highly anticipated]. They said the grass was going to come at a certain day, so then people, in order to agitate, would say, "Do you know that people who live on the odd side are going to get their grass first?" And they said no…

Vern Walentiny: I don't know who started that stuff.

Marge Walentiny: We did! So then [the people across the street] were mad, they'd fight and then they'd call, and well, that's not true. But then pretty soon the people on the even side said, "We heard that we're getting it first and it's going to be on the other side of town where *we* live." Of course, there was a lot of fighting going on over who was going to get the grass first. It didn't take that long, everybody had grass, and they did both sides of the street at once.

Marie Frey*: Silver Bay was very bare. In fact, when we first came here, there was no sidewalk or any sod on the ground. I remember, we didn't have doorbells in the houses. It took three men to put them in: One was in the house listening, another was outside ding-donging, and the third man was writing out the report. They went from house to house to check the doorbells. When we first came here, there wasn't anything beyond Edison. It was just all wooded area. I was glad we could get a house on Davis. We only had a choice of two houses, and my husband took a look at one house which had a very steep driveway. He didn't want that one. We have a very nice piece of land with it, and we're satisfied. I remember one time, in particular, I was so thankful he took this house. That he had the foresight. It was in the winter, and I happened to look out the window, and I saw a woman who lived across the street crawling up her driveway on her hands and knees, because she couldn't make it any other way, except to crawl on her hands and knees, because of the steep driveway.

Nancy Mismash: When we did finally get a house, there were no streets, so the big deal was when we got curbs. Whee! That was a big deal, and then, in went the streets, and then, when we got sidewalk, wow. And when we got grass, that was another big wonderful thing, when the grass came, because they'd come in and roll out the whole grass and we'd get our yard.

George Starkovich: Everybody had a new home. The driveways were built. They came in and laid all the sod; you didn't have to hire your own sod layers. That was part of the company. Reserve Mining had made a deal with Galbreath to put up all the homes.

All the homes were built by John W. Galbreath and Company. The big construction company was Hunkin Arundel Dixon. That was a big company that was here for many, many, many years. You'd say, "Where does your dad work?" "Oh, my dad works at the plant. Where does your dad work?" "My dad works for Hunkin." Nobody, so to speak, worked for John W. Galbreath. Galbreath was like the holding company for the property and the homes.

All of the homes had steel doors in all the rooms: For bathrooms and bedrooms, there were steel doors. The closet doors in all the homes were steel closet doors. The cabinets—all the kitchen cabinets and upper cabinets and lower cabinets—were all steel, and they were all made by Republic Steel. In fact, they had a Republic Steel stamp on them, so the town definitely had all the earmarks of being owned lock, stock, and barrel by Armco and Republic Steel or Reserve Mining Company. Steel garages, as well.

Maggie King: All of the houses' windows were steel, and they were really tough to maintain. They bled all winter long, and it was really a bad part of the architecture.

Anne Przybilla: Another interesting aspect is the actual housing and what the pay was for that. When we lived in the apartments, it was $88 a month. Now they would be called townhouses, because when you see townhouses now, they remind me of that. Then we bought a house up on Ives Road, and we talked about it, because we were going from $88 a month to $94 a month, and that $94 a month covered your house payment, your insurance, the escrow on the loan, everything, and you didn't have a down payment. You had to save $250 for the closing costs, and that was it.

Art Przybilla: The day we moved out, I said, "We can take this key and throw it in the middle of the kitchen floor. Don't worry about selling the place. We haven't lost a nickel."

Ken Pellett: At that time, John W. Galbreath was the housing company that owned all the homes, including the shopping center. At that time our home was, taxes and insurance, $69 a month, for 30 years. We bought our home from a private party that worked at the plant, and I paid him money down and bought the original contract and started making the same payment. At that time, we gave this party a thousand dollars down and started, and it was an original contract.

Harry Holmer: I did the same thing. When they were on that big strike in '59, I bought that house. He said, "You pay the back payments, the house is yours." It was five payments. Five payments of $62, and take over the payments.

Malvin Robinson*: John W. Galbreath, that took care of the house payments, had a house on Davis as an office for quite a few years.

Helen Robinson*: What was nice was when we moved up here, we didn't have to have a down payment on our homes. We could just start making payments. When we moved to Ives, it was $85 a month, and that was your house payment, your taxes, and your insurance.

Ruth Koepke: A lot of the workers were farmers; they didn't have a nickel in their pocket when they came here and were totally amazed when they could buy a house with no money down—actually the payments were less than rent would be. I know our first house cost $87.50.

We first lived in the trailer court. So many workers didn't have places to live. We lived five years in a 28-foot trailer—didn't have bumpouts then, either. And I had one child in that. But the trailer court was big, and then they built the second trailer court. The trailers got bigger then, too. Then we moved from Drake Circle, with no basement, up onto Hays, and our payments were $96 a month, where they were $56. I thought, "Oh my goodness. I don't know how we're going to do that."

Betty Oslund: They sold [residential lots] for $200 for years and years and years. I don't know what they were in the beginning. Maybe everybody bought them with houses on them. That couldn't have factored into the cost of the house at all. For many, many years they remained at $200, which really was nothing for a lot.

Chuck Kaiser: I can't remember the exact year, but I leased a pickup truck, got it out of the Cities, out of one of the suburbs down there and did all this over the phone. A guy ordered the truck and got it, and he called me, and he says, "Okay I got your truck for you, now I'll have to ask some final questions." So he asked, "Do you own your own house?" And I said, "Yeah." He says, "How much do you pay a month?" And it was like $88, and I said, "Of course, that includes taxes, insurance, principal and interest," and it was just dead silence. He actually thought I was lying to him.

Bob Oslund: I think it was $55 we paid when we first come here, and that was everything—taxes, the insurance, and the whole property.

Ruth Koepke: When we lived in the trailer court, we paid $6.50 a month. We paid, I think that was our electricity also. Yeah, $6.50. $5 rent to the company, and a dollar and a half school tax.

Matt Banovetz: Real estate taxes in Babbitt and Silver Bay are reduced due to the company's influence years ago with the legislature, getting legislation passed so that it relieved a lot of the burden on the community. I suppose now some of the politicians wish they had changed it.

Bob Oslund: [Now] you've got a bunch of people who come and buy these houses for recreation houses.

Ruth Koepke: And I don't mind when they called them a summer home, but when they call them a hunting shack, yeah, I take offense at that. Those are our houses, and they've made us very comfortable.

CHAPTER 3

RESIDENTS

With Reserve Mining Company's managers and executives hailing primarily from the East and laborers migrating mainly from rural areas in Minnesota and Wisconsin, Silver Bay had a distinctive mix of cultures. Differences were magnified by echeloning in the housing and other aspects of life in the city. Nevertheless, there were similarities. Because virtually no one was from the immediate area, few considered it "home." At first, many would spend their working days in Silver Bay and then immediately drive to their hometowns for weekends. In addition, most residents were young, newly married, and starting families. Massive numbers of children brought neighbors together more quickly and more often than might otherwise have been the case. Consequently, Silver Bay developed a larger "family" feeling, with the positive and negative aspects of support and scrutiny found in many small cities being amplified by demographic factors. The company contributed to the family-like personality of the city with its own focus on neighborliness and good citizenship. The steelworkers' union also gave a distinctive character to the city.

Betty Oslund: I was thinking, when this company town started, you had a group of people that came from New York, and they were the managers at the plant. Then you've got the farmers from Minnesota and North Dakota and people that had just come out of the service, I assume, who had all these different skills and got jobs here. I really think that they had to learn how to get along together, because they had two different ways of life—from two different parts of the country—and then you add in the fact that one is the managerial class and older for the most part, in their 50s, and then you take the young people who are just starting out with their skills, whether it's welding or whatever, and they're 25 years old, that's quite different. They had to learn how to live together, and I think for the first ten years that caused some problems, and then later on they were able to work it out. It happened in the churches, in the school system, and in the community as a whole.

Tom Malmo: The thing I remember is this was a caste system. If you were in the upper couple, you had a certain place to live, and it would go down to where we merchants were considered scum. It's no joke; it was the truth. You couldn't go here, you couldn't go there, you couldn't do this, you couldn't do that. You can't imagine how it has changed since that day.

Wayne Johnson: I think a lot of that was blown out of proportion. I know out at the golf course they had someone spread the story that only Reserve executives could go out there. Well, the one guy that lived in Beaver Bay, probably a guy on the lowest ranks at Reserve, he was out there playing golf all the time.

Delores Johnson: I think those things were said before those people used to be out there, though, because I do remember they used to say that. Still today that's the reason that the country club doesn't go like they used to, because of that stigma. It's still brought up.

Bob Kind: It's still there but it's lessening a lot.

Lucy Malmo: Well, I think the women were a little snooty about who they were golfing with, or who came out, or if they had lunch with this group or the other group. They weren't all sitting together.

Tom Malmo: Well, there were a few people that wouldn't sign up, but then they expected, because they were of the higher echelon in the company, they should just be put ahead of those people that had made the effort to sign up. You know, a lot of that crap going on.

George Starkovich: Yeah, it was definitely a finger-in-the-eye type of thing. Now, I was virtually in every house on top of the hill and every house down on the other end of town as well as the houses on Floyd Circle, so I was friends with all those kids. I never thought that those kids thought they were special. But some of my classmates say that I am full of baloney because they said, "Well hey, that was you. You were the big man on campus." I think there were probably cliques in school like there is any place, and maybe some kids felt excluded like they do everyplace.

Bob Kind: There was [a caste system]. But some of us didn't pay any attention to that. We went and joined the country club and that was just like a gift. We didn't pay attention to that caste system, and we got along pretty good with both sides. Even if it was a caste system at one time, it's pretty well gone now.

Lucy Malmo: I felt that way, too. We just didn't pay any attention to the company levels. We just had friends—whomever—you know?

Tootie LeBlanc: Now, we weren't employees of Reserve, so therefore there wasn't any discrimination as far as where you're working at. We had it pretty nice, because then we belonged to the country club, and we did whatever. There was no, "You can't be here," or whatever.

Ken Pellett: If you were an hourly employee, you supposedly weren't supposed to associate with salary people.

Mickey Lorntson: I worked in the department that did that plowing, and the driveway cleaning [for certain company officials]. The last five years, I was in charge of it, and I was really into it. Every day someone would come and say, "Can you get me on the plow list? You know, my driveway, I need my driveway plowed." I said, "I can't do that, you gotta get that from somebody else." If the list comes to me and says you're on it, I'll plow it. All kinds of rigamarole trying to get on it. At the end there, before they finally shut it off, we were plowing 43 separate driveways in town.

They had a sign on their garage: It was a little square emblem with a little red dot or something.

Ken Pellett: It was common practice, and I worked in yards and docks, and when it came to snow removal time, if you had a red diamond over your garage door, we plowed your driveway. Otherwise we didn't.

Harry Holmer: It was, pull into Arthur Circle, all of Floyd, all the houses on the top of the hill by the guest house. There must've been 40 houses. We'd plow 40 houses. It took two loaders the whole day.

Mickey Lorntson: You could talk to this one that could talk to that one, and the first thing you know, that one was added, and if he got added, the neighbor couldn't stand that, you know, got to be pretty much equals.

Maggie King: About five houses away was Bob Lee, who was a vice president, and I didn't envy them a bit, because they would make this monstrous mountain right in the front of their front windows. There were years, there were decades where there was a tremendous amount of snow. It wouldn't happen with a snowblower; it'd only happen with that kind of front-end loaders, because you get it all piled up in one place.

Ken Pellett: [If there was] a party out at the country club [with foremen or executives, and it started to snow], call the yards and docks, and away they'd go. It didn't make any difference if it was day or night.

Mickey Lorntson: And then there was one step above that where you got your lawn mowed. The top managers had that.

Ken Pellett: Oh yes, there was some of that, too. We had one hourly employee who worked for the president six months out of the year. In the wintertime, he'd come back to the yards and docks. He mowed the lawns at the guest house and some of the bigger homes.

George Starkovich: Some of the people in town referred to [Arthur Circle] as Silk Stocking Row, because there were some of the nicest homes in town. Up on the upper end, there were some nice homes, too, and that was up on the hill. And there were various names given to that area—Snob Hill, Snob's Knob, or whatever. They give names to various areas depending upon what they hear at the supper table. It was by design that different people of their status in the plant had different housing.

Evie Buetow: That was called Snob Hill because it was all company-built houses and all the officials of the company lived up there, all set—signed, sealed, and delivered. We're the only ones who bought our own lot and built our own house. All of a sudden, this Snob Hill started coming, and that lasted a long time. It went on forever, and that was really hard for the kids. [Our son] Eric came home from grade school one day, and here we had built the house, our furnishings were barely there because we took out lots of loans, and we couldn't just go and build a big house that we wanted. We had orange crates for a table in the dining room. He came home from school one day and blew my mind by asking me, "Mom, are we rich? And what does 'Snob Hill' mean?" So I said a little prayer and said, "Help me. Help me." So I started talking about, "Well, we're rich in many things—the family, nature surrounding us, and all these wonderful things, but no, financially, money in the bank, no." "But why are they calling me this? Saying I live on Snob Hill." Well that's really hard to explain. But that was a problem for a long, long, long time.

Art Przybilla: A quirky story was around for a long time and actually from Bob Granger: He was the principal of the high school, and when he was going to build a house, he wanted to build up on Snob Hill, and they wouldn't let him. They wouldn't sell him a lot up there, but a high school principal could be halfway up the hill. So he was halfway up the hill.

Ed Hynes: There seemed to be a division there, when I got a little extra here and there, of the benefits. It seemed to cut off some people, not everybody, but just a few would drift away from you.

Lois Hynes: They just kind of acted like we felt we were better because we built on the hill.

George Pope: I think the kids at the schools didn't sense the caste system, unless we went into the houses. The executive houses were like palaces compared to 34E Bell Circle and 61 Burk.

Rose Elam: It depends on who you've talked to, too, they'll say, "Well my kids were never accepted into that group," or you know.

Matt Banovetz: Earldyne Begich, who still lives in the apartments in Silver Bay, was [my wife] Ilona's best friend. A lot of people couldn't understand how Earldyne and Ilona could be such good friends because of my position. People got to know each other through time. I think our children, although our kids never complained, I suspect that there were times when people would needle them because of my job.

It was always my feeling that whatever title I became, I was still the same person, and I certainly didn't think that I was any better, and I would think that this is probably true in most corporations. I liken my position—my life—to a Ferris wheel. You get on, you can't stop. It just keeps going, and the next thing you know you got another job and another job and another job. The next thing you know, you look back, and everybody's reporting to you. But my wife and I certainly didn't feel better than anybody, and, consequently, I think people accepted us, as we were and didn't necessarily stand off.

I grew up in a family where my dad was an ironworker. My dad seldom ever talked about the superintendent without calling him an S.O.B. To the extent that when I became a supervisor I almost hesitated to tell my parents that I was a foreman, because now I was no longer a union person. There were some people unfortunately that got promoted to be foremen who all of a sudden felt that it made them better than the rest of the people, which was a great mistake on their part, and it made it very difficult for them. I think that the relationship between the salaried people and the hourly people improved through time.

Carol Roeben: I can remember when [my husband, Clarence] started out and then became a foreman, I got a whole series of different phone calls, because people would say, "Well your husband's a foreman. You have to join the country club, you have to do this." And I kept saying, "No I don't." I never did, and they said, "But you have to," and they would try and try. You know, "Oh come for coffee here." I said, "I'm sorry, but my friends were my friends long before he had the foreman's job, so they're still my friends."

Mickey Lorntson: Everyone that worked [at Reserve] had a hard hat, and depending on what their job was, it was a certain color. All the foremen's were orange. Regardless of what kind of a job they were doing, electrical foremen's were orange, maintenance foremen's were orange. But maintenance personnel's were white, electricians were yellow, the instrument repairmen's were, I think, red, pelletizer personnel were green, concentrators were blue. All the managers had orange, down as far as the shift foreman. Pretty much everyone that had an orange hat was a salaried person.

Matt Banovetz: That's true, yeah: Pumpkin heads. I never could understand that. They had different color for electricians, for maintenance, mechanics, for operators, for supervisors, and I never could understand why they needed to have a different color hat. Just like the housing separation, didn't help a bit in cooperation.

Dick King: The story was that some of the ladies would get one of those helmets and put it so everybody could see it when they were driving around.

Ken Pellett: There was the blue collar worker and the white collar. Nobody knew for sure in the salaried people how much they made. That was a secret deal. They asked me one time if I wanted to be a step-up foreman. And at the time I said, "Well I have to know." They said, "Well we can't tell you to start with." Well I said, "If you think I'm gonna take the job not knowing what I might get, you're crazy." I mean, that's common sense. But salary people pretty much stuck together, and the hourly people were, we were on our own.

Mary Stahovic*: Mr. Furness came to the clinic one day and asked Stanley if he would take a foremen's job. He had talked to him, and then he came up to talk to me at the clinic, and I says, "Mr. Furness, Stanley is happy where he is at." Stanley had said that if he took a foreman's cap, once he put that orange cap on, he wouldn't have the rapport that he had with the employees, the other men. He said he liked it the way it was. I said, "I'm working, why should he take a headache job?" Mr. Furness had asked me, and I said, "No!" I told him right out.

Ken Pellett: At that time, this was strictly a union operation. It was very interesting to be a part of it, because they run 24/7, 365 days a year.

Arlene Pellett: Every four years, a contract came through. That was a stressful time for people, because you didn't know if it was going to be settled, or if they were going to go on strike.

Ken Pellett: It was quite interesting because I came here in spring of '59, and I believe it was July 1, and we went on strike. I'd just gotten my feet on the ground, bought a car. We were out for four months, I believe. We didn't come back to work 'til fall. We all just disappeared and had to look for other work. We've gone through several strikes. Some have lasted awhile, but that was the worst one. I went one year to the University of Wisconsin, to one of their camps out in the wilderness, and another year I went to an outfit building turkey barns down in Wisconsin, out by Rice Lake, and there was about six of us who went on that job. Whenever you found a job, you'd come back and holler at any of your friends or buddies, "You wanna work?"

Arlene Pellett: The good thing about the strike in '59 was that's when [my husband and I] met, really. My parents and his grandparents knew each other from before, because they were both rural mail carriers, so they kind of knew the families. We met because he came back to our area to work while the strike was going on up here.

Harry Holmer: I hauled cookies during the strike of '59. I hauled cookies for four months. A dollar an hour. That's all we got.

Ed Hynes: Early on, there was a strike, and nobody had much equity in their homes because they didn't have a down payment, they just started making payments. Every now and then, somebody would just put a note on their front door saying, "I'm gone. Take it back." And they'd just walk away from it.

Pat LeBlanc: This was a good crew they had here. A lot of the times when they went on those strikes and the guys went someplace else and worked, the guys where they went wanted them to stay because they were good men. There was a lot of that.

Evie Buetow: We had some pretty good, long strikes. That was really hard not only on Reserve people but on the businesspeople, because the dentist was the last one that got paid. I'll never forget this one nice, nice lady had a big family, and how it came out I don't remember, but many, many years later she told Harry, she'll never forget, because they had a big family and big dental bills, and she wrote out a check every month for $5. He never charged interest. Whatever they could pay, or if they couldn't pay for a long time, and she remembered that.

Anne Przybilla: Unions were something that I read about in history books, and then we moved to a company town. I remember [a neighbor across the street from the apartments] saying, "We are just now getting our heads above water." She said, "This is our breakeven month." And I said, "What do you mean, your breakeven month?" She said, "From the strike." And evidently, there was a big strike like in 1959. This was in 1962, and she said they were just back financially at the place where they had been when that strike began, and I have never forgotten that.

Ruth Koepke: Unions had their place, but there was a lot of hard feelings between company and union. There was a very big distinction between the hard hat colors. I'm so thankful today that our plant is non-union, because they get along so much better.

George Starkovich: When you were hired, you were given this brass tag, heavy brass tag, about the size of a dollar bill, maybe not a dollar bill, a silver dollar. It was about twice as thick, and it had a number stamped in it, and there was a loop or hole in the top, and you could attach that to a watch fob or whatever, but when you went in and out of that gate, you were supposed to show your brass.

Ruth Koepke: My dad had the number-one badge at Reserve Mining, he was the first one hired. He was non-union and lived out his time at Reserve Mining, so we got a good education watching everything happen here. When he retired, they made a plaque with his badge, with the number one on it.

George Starkovich: The gate guards could pull you aside and go through your car, and they'd ask you to open up your lunch bucket, things of that sort. The reason being that some people would steal tools—everything was first class down at Reserve. They had the first-class tools and this and that and the other thing. The construction was working down there, and everything was not secured, so there were stories that there were some people that were caught trying to sneak a bottle of acetylene out of the plant there or this, that and the other thing. So the plant was guarded very vociferously by the people that were down there. They were called plant protection. They not only watched the gate, but they also had patrol cars, and they would patrol the various areas that were owned by Reserve Mining Company.

Bob Eckstrom: Well, you were talking about unions, but they're a necessary evil. Because they're right in here because other people are in the union to keep the wages up or they wouldn't be. Another thing about the union: We don't have every summer off like the schoolteachers, but we do get 13 weeks once every five years. We didn't know when we'd get that 13 weeks. If it was during the winter, we'd get the feel for school, kids would go and get their assignments for the whole 13 weeks, and we'd go different places—go through a sugar factory, go through mints, Denver, Colorado—education all the way around—go into Mexico and come back, and we'd get back the last day.

Walter Skalsky*: The union was great. In fact, when I first started working for the [Susquehanna] mine [near Hibbing], we started the union. We used to meet in basements of taverns. But, like anything else, they had bad apples, and we had quite a few of them in Silver Bay.

Karl Jevning*: [In a union plant], if you had a burned out bulb, you couldn't touch that bulb. You had to call an electrician to change that bulb for you. At home, you screw out the bulb and put in a new one. There were things that were irritating, but the union had its place. I was glad I belonged to it. I was a grievance man for a period of time, and this kind of turned me off, too. I was to represent someone and they wanted me to lie to supervision about some of the activities that had been going on, which I would not do, and that kind of upset them, so that kind of turned me off. All the people in the union were not that way. We had good people in there, too, but it doesn't take too many to sour things. Without the union in the steel industry, it's hard telling what our company would have been like. So, I'm glad they were there and glad for the good things they did do.

We were a clicky bunch. Us in the pelletizer would hardly associate with anybody from the concentrator and those from the main office were strictly taboo.

Fran Jevning*: But, that feeling was promoted by the plant at that time. They didn't want their people to associate with the common worker. That wasn't promoted by the people themselves. The people themselves were loving, kind, ordinary people, but there was that class separation, and that was an unfortunate thing.

Karl Jevning*: People from my department would stick together right or wrong, and so did other departments. That's gone by the wayside now.

Fran Jevning*: I don't know if they thought their word would carry more clout or weight if they were a separate group or something. It was unfortunate there was that separation because of position.

Karen Bock: Well when you went to a dance at the union hall, I mean it was electricians at this table and the mechanics at this table, and that's kind of how it was at every dance.

Rose Elam: The people you got to know were those your husband worked with, so that's who you got to be friends with, so that's who you sat with.

Donna Beaupre: When they filmed *Iron Will* in Two Harbors, I talked to a gal that I'd worked with at the bank who lived up here, and she said very definitely the foremen didn't mix with the regular workers. My dad worked down at yards and docks, a custodian. [My parents] never talked about it, but there was the definite caste system.

Rose Elam: [Some of] the first people that [my husband] Beech got to know and then I got to know were promoted to foreman. When they got to be foremen, I don't think he lost any friends. He was never foreman, he was just a welder—not just a welder, he was a good welder!

Evie Buetow: I didn't understand all this going on around about this hierarchy or whatever you call it, so I just did the thing that my mother would've taught me to do: You reciprocate the kindnesses. We lived on this little slab house on Banks Boulevard, and I picked up the phone one day and called Mrs. Kelley [the company president's wife] and invited them for dinner. Wow! How dare I? A friend of mine, a good friend of mine, whose husband worked for the plant, had called and wanted me to go to Two Harbors that day. And I said, "I can't, I'm having company for dinner." She asked, "Who?" I said, "Well, Mr. and Mrs. Kelley." "You WHAT?!" And she actually said, "How did you dare?" I said, "What do you mean, 'dare?' I just picked up the phone and asked them, and she accepted with pleasure." So they came. I had a drop-leaf table in the living room that I could set—a nicer table than in the little kitchen. I cooked a pretty darn good meal, and I'll never forget what she told me when they left. She thanked us so much for inviting them into our home, because she said, "You're the first people and the only people that have done this." She said, "People are afraid to invite us because [others would say] they were brown-nosing or something."

Ed Hynes: They must've felt isolated.

Evie Buetow: Well that's what she said, this was so pleasant, "We would like to get to know the people better, but they're all afraid."

Evelyn Turonie: It continued for a lot of years afterward, because, for some reason or other, Pat Bryant latched on to me. We were invited to dinner there and everything, but the people around town would say, "How do you rate?"

Lois Hynes: Well they said the same thing to me when Jane Gosnell [her husband, a plant executive] and I were golfing buddies, and I had to go to Duluth one day, so she said, "Well I'll take care of Leslie." And I didn't know anybody around to be a babysitter or anything. Well they just had a fit when they heard that Jane Gosnell was taking care of my child—like having the queen look after my child.

Tim Bjella: I never knew that, and I never cared. I had to talk to, I think it was Ed Furness, he was the president. Actually, I was dealing with some money from the company, and I called him up, talked to his secretary and then told her what I needed. I talked to Ed for a little bit. The next day I talked to one of their guys, and I said, "I talked to Ed about this." And he said, "You didn't talk to Ed." I said, "Yeah, I talked to Ed." He said, "Nobody talks to Ed." But I didn't know that he was next to God up there, so it didn't make any difference to me.

Evie Buetow: Going back to where we built our house, where it was fashioned out of solid rock. There was all these rock piles out in front. And it was before they filled it in with dirt and sod and everything, so there was this little hill full of rock. And then there were supposed to be some steps up to our porch that weren't there yet. So we had these two broad boardwalks going from the porch all the way to where it leveled off by the driveway. Well, here we go again with the president of the company at that time. This was after Mr. Kelley was gone. They came from New York: the Furness family, that'd be Jane, and then there was Doris. They had been raised in schools in Switzerland or something—I mean, a whole different way of life. There they were, at the top of the heap. Jane was pretty down to earth and didn't do all this entertaining and everything, so I knew her vaguely but not really well. I ran into her in the grocery store one day, and we were at that point in our house with just the boardwalk. Because she knew we where we'd built our house, she made a big deal out of saying, "Well when are we going to be invited for tea?" And Doris was with her, and this other gal, her sister from New York, and I just took them up on it right away. I said, "How about tomorrow morning at 10:00, come on out for coffee." So the next morning, this car drives up at 10:00, I've got my jeans on and a sweatshirt, and the three get out all dressed. High heel shoes and white gloves and hats and carrying purses; they had to trip trop up my boardwalk because they were coming to 7 Kent Lane on Snob Hill for morning coffee. I didn't know what to think at first. I said, "Oh my, what is this?" Well the minute they came in the front hall, off came the hats—they'd made their impression—off came the hats and gloves and shoes and everything. They were pulling the big high society thing. A good sense of humor, anyway.

Pat LeBlanc: I gotta tell you this: You know I was rolling around delivering fuel all day, every day. I knew everybody and where they lived and what they drove for cars—how much they made even, almost. I knew everybody and where they lived, and I never had to look it up. When I'd meet somebody from out of town, I'd tell them I wrote the phonebook. You could tell me a name, and I could give you an address; you give me an address, I'd give you a name.

Arlene Pellett: I was a teacher in Wisconsin in 1955 to 1960. I moved up here to Silver Bay in 1961, and we bought a home at 38 Adams Boulevard, and we're still there. Raised two daughters, and this was a unique place to raise a family. You knew all of your neighbors, and they knew all your kids. They treated your kids like their own; if they were doing something wrong, they reprimanded them.

George Starkovich: The other thing is, this thing that came out a few years ago, "It takes a whole village to raise a child." Well, it wasn't anything new; it was just never touted as a phrase before. If I was downtown playing in Morris McInerney's yard with some of the boys, and we started messing around, and I threw a rock through Mrs. McInerney's window, guess what? Mrs. McInerney was on the phone to Mr. Starkovich, and when I got home, we had a big discussion about it. If I were playing in the neighborhood, and we started getting a little loud or we were cussing and swearing out there, and there were little kids in the neighborhood, the neighbors thought nothing of coming out and saying, "Hey, you guys watch your mouth out there. We're not gonna take this." Back in those days, if you were on your bicycle, your flat-wheel bicycle, flat-tire bicycle messing around the front door or the shopping center and impeding the progress of people that were coming out, nobody would be afraid to say, "Hey, you kids, move your bicycles and get the heck out of here, you know this is a business."

Arlene Pellett: It was kind of unique in a way, and yet it took awhile to actually call this home, because just about everybody was from somewhere else and had moved up here. On Friday nights, it was kind of like the exodus, because everybody went back home [to their hometowns], even though this was home, or a lot of us did, anyway, to see our families.

Evelyn Turonie: We moved here in 1954. Our son was in the first grade, and our daughter was younger than that. I remember the teachers disliked the schedule at Reserve because they would get four days off on a week, long weekend, if they came off of midnights and went on to some other shift. And the teachers hated it, because the kids were gone, this kid was gone one week, this one was gone another week, and they were always behind on attendance.

Arlene Pellett: I remember when, [my husband] worked usually days and afternoon shifts. He'd come home at 11:00 off the afternoon shift, and sometimes we'd go snowmobiling with our neighbors.

George Starkovich: They had three shifts: "afternoons," 3:00–11:00; "midnights,"11:00–7:00; and "days," 7:00–3:00—so, at about 2:30, people would start coming into the plant for the 3:00 shift change. At about 3:02 to 3:10, there'd be a line of cars trying to get out of the plant, and again at 10:30 people would start coming in, and 6:30 in the morning they'd start coming in. You'd see this big line of cars coming in and out of the plant.

Ken Pellett: Most generally, the top four or five fellows had a choice. In the yards and docks we worked around the clock, but you could work days and afternoons, and depending how much you wanted to make, you could work weekends, and they either took off Friday/Saturday or Sunday/Monday, but usually the older fellows took straight days. I was always sold on days and afternoons because I absolutely did not like midnights. We changed every week, and that was a big drawback. So if you'd get used to straight midnights, it'd be alright, but days and afternoons I liked, because I did get a chance to see the kids occasionally.

Arlene Pellett: When he was on afternoon shift, our girls didn't usually see him for a week because they were at school, and when they got home, he was gone to work.

Ed Hynes: The one thing that I think makes this town unique: Everybody was from someplace else. I think that made a difference in the town's personality.

Malvin Robinson*: At one time, there were 17 [of us] families from Chetek that were up here.

Ed Hynes: Our friends came from New York, some from Kentucky, Wisconsin, the Dakotas. The first thing you ask anybody: "Where ya' from?" A lot of people, on weekends, they'd go home. This wasn't home yet. It took awhile for this to become home.

Clarence Roeben: There's a lot of hands, and a lot of faces, and lots of them from Duluth, Two Harbors, up and down the Shore. And people, when they talk about going back home, Frederick, Wisconsin, Siren, and up at Danbury is what they talk about—where they came from. Lots and lots of boys came off the farm and put things together.

Karen Bock: They all went "home" for the weekends. This was where they worked and lived during the week, but they went "home" on the weekends to their hometowns. This was a paydate. They didn't really want to make it home, this place was where they lived and made their money.

Ruth Koepke: Nobody called it home at first. The churches were pretty empty on Sunday, because everybody went home. And there's people today that still say [they are going home], and I say, "You're going where? Home is where you hang your hat."

Fran Jevning*: Everybody here was fresh-off-the-farm type, and they came to work Monday through Friday, and as soon as they got their days off, it was shooom out of here, they were going "home" until they had to come back to work. This was just a temporary place to go and work and get your paycheck and go "home." But as the years went by, now this is home. We've been here for over half of our lives, and this is home and has been home to us. Neither one of us would ever think of, if we lost each other, I would never go back to Tennessee. To what? This is home: This is where we met and fell in love, married, had our child, made our home, so the security in home base is here, not somewhere else. At that time, it was not. It was a very temporary stop for everybody. It wasn't thought of as a permanent place.

Tom Langley: I had a paper route when I was in the eighth or ninth grade. I got to know the people so well, but so many people moved in and out. I mean, it was a really transient, I'd go to collect and they were gone, I mean, they didn't just try to stiff me, but you know, they didn't think, "I'll leave money for the paperboy." People were really coming and going.

Tim Bjella: The year that we started teaching here, my wife and I were going to UMD. I was working on my master's, so we got to visit with people who were living on the Shore who were familiar with the area. My wife came home one time and said, "You know what kind of town Silver Bay is." We hadn't spent any time there yet. She says, "Pretty wild. They have a lot of parties. There's wife swapping. There's kitty clubs." You know what a kitty club is?" And I said, "No." She said, "I'll check on it." And so the next day she came back, she says, "This gal says it's really a wild town." Well, you've gotta believe that, I guess the average age must have been in the mid-20s. And I said, "They can think that if they wanted to." It sounded a little exciting. When we did come here, we would create our own excitement. We'd put on dances, we had a dance club, we had a square dance, that we just did for our own entertainment. There was nothing else. We had a good time, used the union hall, and hired a band and pack the place, but that was the idea.

Karl Jevning*: It wasn't a place you thought you'd work a lifetime at, but as your kids grew up and went to school here, it got to be more stable.

Donna Beaupre: I don't think Silver Bay was like Grand Marais and Two Harbors, if you weren't Swedish, Norwegian, or from there. Silver Bay wasn't like that, because everybody was new.

Evelyn Turonie: We knew all our neighbors in a couple days because of the kids. There were 20 kids in four houses in our neighborhood. There were six to the right, six to the left, and our two, and we had another six. Twenty kids in four houses.

Ed Hynes: Everybody was young and had kids. Our first Halloween, we had over 200 kids come to the door—finally we had to close the doors and turn off the lights.

Tootie LeBlanc: It was just one big family. We lived on Davis Drive. How many little kids were there at that time? There was 46 in one block area. And we moved to Palisade, and there was 28 out in the country. They always had playmates, and they played well. They never had to have toys or anything. You didn't have to worry about them. You didn't have to worry about somebody picking them up off the highway or whatever.

Judy Kaiser: In the '60s, the average age in this town was 39, and the average number of children per family was 4.7.

Jenny Heinzen*: When we moved here with our four kids, there were 97 children on Evans Circle.

Mary Carlson*: We had 82 kids on [our] block. Every block was the same way.

Charles Heinzen*: The average age of the people working at the plant was 32 years old then. And the oldest ones probably weren't over 50.

Mickey Lorntson: The trailer court was just full of kids. All the people that lived there had several kids—little kids. I was a truck driver for the company that was building the plant at the time, and I got an assignment to haul some material out to the upper end of the trailer court because they were digging up a water line. I knew that place was just crawling with kids, and I said, "Before I go there, you can assign me a spotter to back up," because backing over a kid is the easiest thing in the world. So, they did that for me, and I hauled about three or four loads, and I'm driving up through this trailer court, and here's a cardboard box, I suppose about two-and-a-half feet square, maybe a foot-and-a-half high, in my driving lane. Well I, of course, went around it, because you don't want to drive over something that could damage a tire or whatever. And I went past, I looked in the mirror, and there's two little kids in that box. They were playing in that box. It just made my hair stand on end at how close, if I had been another vehicle, I'm not sure what I would've done. Only a box. That was all that I saw, just a box.

Karen Bock: If there was a gray-haired person on the street, it was somebody's grandma and grandpa. It wasn't anybody that lived here. Somebody had a grandma visiting.

Anne Przybilla: Everybody was the same age, everybody was having kids, so there were kids out in strollers, tricycles, all that all the time. But everybody was the same age. I don't think there was anybody over 50 in town.

Evelyn Turonie: I was considered one of the oldest because our son was in the first grade, so every neighbor around, if their kid fell and skinned their knee, they'd come running to me. "What do I do? What do I do?" I was kind of the mother of the neighborhood because I was older.

Chuck Kaiser: There were over 300 school-aged children on Davis, that big loop there, and of course most of them were elementary age at that point. I don't think there was anybody over 40 years old when we moved here.

Lois Hynes: You just knew everybody. When we first moved into the house on Arthur Circle, Ed was working, and I was cleaning and painting and doing some stuff up, and one day there was this big deep voice, "Where's the twins?" I almost fell off the ladder. Two little kids were looking for the twins that had lived in that house. I said, "Well it's fine if you want to come and visit, but knock on the door, don't just walk in." "Okay." So off they went, and before I had met any of the neighbors, the kids said, "There's a lady over there. She's got a pink living room." I was painting [my living room pink], so I was the lady with the pink living room before anybody met me.

Judy Kaiser: It was interesting how in this town it's like we knew everybody. I can remember, we were just in town a couple years, and I wanted to fix the house up a little bit on Davis. We had one car, and [my husband] Chuck had it at school [where he worked], and I called down to Jacobsons' [Hardware] and told them that I needed this paint and that Chuck would pick it up after school. Well, about an hour later, Roy delivered it.

Lois Hynes: Maury Flannigan delivered the mail, and we were going to be out of town for awhile, so I went down to the office and picked up Ed's check. A few days after we got back, Maury was so concerned because his check wasn't in the mail. I said, "Well I went and picked it up." Maury just watched things like that.

Judy Kaiser: This is a funny story because of the way that Maury was, he knew everybody's mail: Chuck and his friend Jerry Rude took their motorcycles, and they went up to Ely. Chuck sent me this postcard from there, just like it was from somebody else, and he didn't sign it. Maury, the next day, asked, "Do you have friends living away from here?" He wanted to know about that postcard!

Carol Roeben: One day we had some fresh-from-the-garden rutabagas and carrots, and I'm peeling them away, and then this thing comes on on the radio or the television or something about wasting vitamins, right? So I thought, oh alright, this is all fresh, I'm going to throw all these peelings into a kettle and make some soup stock, right? So that night when we were eating, I told the kids that I had made this from the carrot peelings and the rutabaga skins. And you couldn't see them, they were totally dissolved—they didn't know. Well, our daughter went to school the next day, and she got into home ec, and she says, "My mom made soup out of the peelings." Do you know I got a phone call the next day? "Well Mrs. Roeben, we have social services that will…" I mean, if anybody should know anything about vitamins in the food, it should be the home ec teacher.

Anne Przybilla: I was the president of the PTA one year, and Fran Jevning, who was the policewoman in town at the time, came knocking on our door, and she had a tape measure with her. She said, "I'm here to measure your skirts." And I said, "Excuse me?" She said, "I don't think it's right for anyone in your position to wear such short skirts." Now, I was never really a fashion lady, and I never wore skirts that short, although at school, there was a dress code then: If you were kneeling down, your skirt had to touch the floor. I said, "What dress are you talking about?" And she said, "You know that plaid suit that you wear with that pleated skirt. It's too short, and I want you to put it on and measure it right now." [My husband] wasn't home, and the kids are there, and I said, "Okay." So I put it on, and I said, "You know, the dress code at school is you have to kneel down." I knelt down, and the skirt didn't just touch the floor, it was about an inch longer than that. So I said, "What's the deal?" "I still think it's too short," [she said], and I never heard anything more about it.

Lorraine Rustari*: Living in a town with most of my contemporaries married was not the ideal situation, nor was the small town syndrome of having your private life scrutinized. The big city beckoned me back many times, but with camera in hand, I learned to love the beauty of the North Shore, nature at my back door, with brooks and trees and birds and friends, and so I remained and consider myself almost a pioneer.

George Starkovich: A lot of memories go by when I think of my times here in Silver Bay from the dirt roads and board sidewalks to the games that we played between upper town and lower town, and the wonderful people that we had. The unique thing about Silver Bay is that it always has stuck together. My father, for example, was stricken with end-stage renal disease, his kidneys failed, so he had to be put on dialysis, and that meant that he would have to make three or four trips a week to Duluth. That's kind of a daunting task. Some of the professionals down there said, "Well maybe it would be better if you moved to Duluth." He did not want even to think about leaving Silver Bay. To help our family solve that problem, there was a cadre of volunteers in this community that drove him four times a week for 12 years to get his dialysis treatments. They took it upon themselves to volunteer, no cost to my family, to drive him down, and he had a four-hour treatment. They'd drop him off, and then they'd pick him up, so literally speaking, they'd give up one of their days to spend with my father so he could receive treatment and help him along the way until his death.

Lois Hynes: You always felt like you had somebody watching over you.

Ken Pellett: We always said we led a very sheltered life.

Pat LeBlanc: We did. It was a very good start for everybody.

CHAPTER 4

BUSINESSES & AMENITIES

During Silver Bay's earliest years of existence, residents went shopping in Two Harbors or Duluth for all but the most basic items. Once Reserve Mining Company had the local "shopping center" built and sold it to John W. Galbreath, the city acquired a simultaneously varied and limited collection of stores meant to provide for the needs of the plant's employees. Small business growth was severely limited by the availability of real estate for that purpose. Also, with most residents being employed at the plant, there was virtually no focus on economic diversification or on attracting outside customers or tourists to the city. At the same time, the company provided some amenities unseen elsewhere, including a golf course and country club, a commissary for public events, doctors with a clinic open to the public, rescue squad and firefighting equipment, land for churches, and more.

Wayne Johnson: I first came up in here in 1951. I was working for an insurance adjusting firm, and this was part of my territory. I could see that there was going to be a big development here. There was a lot of optimism; people were looking forward to good jobs. When I got out of law school and went into the practice in 1952, I decided to come up here because I thought there would be good opportunities. I tried to get space in Silver Bay, and there just wasn't any available, so I set up the law office in Beaver Bay and was there until 1956, when they built the Norshor Building. Since that was a private enterprise, I was able to get lots of space in the building. I also wanted to buy a lot to build a home, but they would not sell lots to anyone who was not Reserve workers or employees. So I built a little building in Beaver Bay and had my law office there until 1956.

Lucy Malmo: [My husband] Tom's dad came up here, and we moved up here at the same time, but when we decided to open up the store, they made us take the store up in Babbitt, too, the drugstore. We couldn't just come and open a drugstore here. They were very selective. They wouldn't let people just come in and open a business; you had to follow just exactly the way they wanted it to be. There were a lot of regulations about things.

Tom Malmo: They started regulating what you could carry and what you couldn't sell and things like that.

Lucy Malmo: We had a nice rental system. If you sold a little more merchandise, then you paid a little more rent. It wasn't a flat rent; if you did more business, then they collected a little more, so it was a percentage.

Wayne Johnson: The people that built the Norshor Building were the insurance agents for Armco and Republic out in Middletown, Ohio. That's the reason they came here. They wanted an office building, so they bought that lot and built the Norshor Building. My brother was in the dry cleaning business; we arranged for him to buy the lot next door, and we kind of slipped that through. The company was not interested in selling to private individuals yet, so the people that built the Norshor

Building agreed that they would buy that lot because they wanted more space. When they got title to it, I arranged for them to turn it over to my brother.

I only met John W. Galbreath once. He came up here and he came in, and at that time I had an office on the top floor. It was a corner office, so it was a beautiful spot, because I could look all over Silver Bay from my office. He came in, and his first comment was, "How did you get this good spot?" Well they had appointed me the building manager, and so I had rented out all the space to all of the offices in the building, so I had the opportunity to select a nice side.

When I was appointed the city attorney, Lynn Brickles was the first mayor. They agreed that I would attend all council meetings and do all the legal work for them. They would pay me the rather handsome sum of $75 a month. That was the way I got started as far as municipal representation was concerned. Fortunately, a lot of people were buying homes. The highway was then very crooked and hilly and there were a lot of accidents. I was getting my business from people who didn't want Reserve's attorney to handle their real estate transactions, so I was successful in handling a very good portion of the sales on homes. Like anybody else in business, it was tough going at first and a lot of my colleagues asked, "Why did you want to come up here and eke out a living when you could've gone into a nice big firm in Minneapolis?" Well, that's what I wanted to do. I was the city attorney for the whole 50 years, so I guess I appreciated what I did.

Evie Buetow: After [my husband] Harry had his [dental] practice in the house for awhile, he was told he had to get out of the house, after putting all that money and making it into a dental office. So the next move was to the first floor of the credit union [the Norshor Building]. When he had to get out of that house, then he had to start all over again and make another dental office, on the first floor. And then eventually later on he moved up to the second floor and had half of the second floor. And that's where he practiced until 1991.

Harry Buetow*: In 1959, after practicing here for years, we had a steel strike, and most people weren't able to pay their bills, and I didn't even send out bills for awhile. It was from July, I think, until December when it was pretty tough for everybody. The most exciting thing that happened in the dental office was in 1976. That is when everybody didn't do anything for six months waiting for the dental insurance to kick in so that the insurance would pay for it. I was on the corner of Banks and Davis, until they built in 1957, the Norshor Building. Then I went upstairs, and that is where I stayed. The liquor store was downstairs from the office. Several times we'd have to either call them up or go down and quiet them down so we wouldn't hear all the noise from the liquor store up through the floor.

Lucy Malmo: When we were first opening, there were a lot of construction people still living here. That was good for our business, because at Christmas they would buy lots of things, and it was good. We were a drugstore, the general store of Silver Bay. Tom sold TVs, and we sold gifts, and we had the flower shop. In the holidays, the counter would be full of poinsettias for Christmas or lilies for Easter, and we sold all the flowers and just about anything. We had clothes, we had yard goods, we just had everything at that time.

Wayne Johnson: About the only thing you didn't have was groceries.

Lucy Malmo: Bernie [Zupancich, the grocer] was very good about not having a lot of over-the-counter meds and things at the grocery store, because he knew that we were carrying those things.

We had a hard time once. It was a union town, and we didn't have the union at the drugstore. [Our] people really didn't want the union, but they were picketing out in front of the store and wanting us to join the union. The workers wouldn't cross the picket line to come in and shop. They wouldn't come in and buy, because people were out watching to keep track of who was crossing the picket line and coming into the store to shop. It was very bad for business at the time.

Wayne Johnson: The first grocery store was set up by Galbreath. The site of the first groceries building was where City Hall is now. It was one of Armco's big steel buildings. Even earlier, there was a small one in one of the first little houses built.

Carol Roeben: Yeah, our first grocery store was on Bell Circle in a garage.

Evelyn Turonie*: It was so crowded, you couldn't meet anybody in an aisle.

Lloyd Houle: And then they moved it out to the city, where City Hall was, before they built the shopping center.

Evelyn Turonie*: When it moved from Bell Circle, there were Quonset huts where city hall is or sort of like Quonset houses.

Wayne Johnson: But it wasn't long after that that they built the big building at the shopping center.

Jenny Heinzen*: I remember the IGA store. It seemed really neat to have all these modern conveniences, to have shopping so close by. That's what my feeling was at the time.

Mary Carlson*: Felix and Ruth Nelson, I think, were the first grocers in the Big Dollar where Zup's is now. Then Sparky [Neil] and Betty McNeil came after them, and then came Zup's. I think that's the way it was.

Marie Frey*: The first grocery store was in at the old municipal building and that was moved over to the shopping center that was built. Next door to that was the bank, where the café is right now. Later on, this is a matter of, I don't know, maybe a couple of years or a year they built the bank. Don Suess, the chief of police borrowed a grocery cart. They piled all the money in the grocery cart and wheeled it over to the present bank. That's how the money was transferred. Who is going to rob anyone up here?

Marge Walentiny: We didn't have a Silver Bay mail address. Everything was Beaver Bay, but we had a post office. They had a house on the corner there, and you went and got your mail. So that's how we got our mail there.

Vern Walentiny: The post office was right behind the clinic parking lot, where the clinic is now.

Marie Frey*: The post office was in a house when we first came here. Then it moved up to part of the present Julie's store. That was the post office. Later, a new post office was built.

Mary Carlson*: And they put Rocky Taconite [by the post office], and then later they took Rocky and put him down by the Veterans Home [corner of Outer Drive and Adams Boulevard].

Ruth Koepke: When they were going to name the mascot to our city, it was either Rocky Taconite or Petey Pellet. Those were the two names that were submitted. I'm thinking Rocky Taconite is better.

Marge Walentiny: They had the liquor store—actually it was a bar—and the town hall in the same building, all together, so you could be having a highball while you were paying for your taxes.

Vern Walentiny: Kind of where the City Hall is now, that's where it was sitting. It was one of these old tin buildings.

Marge Walentiny: Nobody thought anything about it. You go in, you have a drink. Might as well pay my water bill at the same time or whatever it was, you know?

Charles Heinzen*: Before that, everybody drove to Two Harbors for their booze.

Marie Frey*: We didn't have a liquor store. The VFW had a clubroom down in the basement of the Norshor Building after that was built. For awhile, that was our liquor store. I always felt that we should never have a lounge, that we should have a store only. We had several votes on this. It was my feeling that we should give out the licenses, as many as we could give out, one, two, or whatever to clubs, Moose, VFW, American Legion, whoever would like to have a license and let them have the business. They could make their money in that way. They could have a restaurant and the city would have a bottle store only. In that way, we would be getting license fees every year and no problems. I wonder if many people know how many lawsuits and problems that we had throughout the years with our liquor lounge.

Ken Pellett: When I came here, the police station was in that big metal building that the city moved up—the mining company moved it up there, and that was the police station and the council chambers.

Marie Frey*: The municipal building went into the old grocery store. It was a long building—I would say roughly 300 feet long. One end was the library. Margaret Davidson was the person responsible to get the library started. She had a library club, and we would review books, and it was very interesting.

Anne Przybilla: My hometown had this wonderful old Carnegie public library, and the library here was a room in this metal building.

Marie Frey*: In the middle part [of the municipal building] was the room that the council members met and the different boards and commissions. The police station, and at the far end was the restrooms and the janitors' room. It was in one long building. Later, when we had a vote go through that we were going to build a new city hall, the old one was put out on bids. The Assembly of God Church in Beaver Bay had the low bid, and the members and minister took that building apart piece by piece and reassembled it in Beaver Bay. That is their present church. Of course, with other brick sidings or whatever they have, but basically, the shell is our old municipal building.

Marge Walentiny: [At first] they didn't have any churches [in Silver Bay], and we had to make do with what we could get. The school in Beaver Bay was available to us on Sundays. So the Catholic people had their masses first, so they would put up the chairs.

Vern Walentiny: They had a portable altar.

Marge Walentiny: But they had an agreement with the Sychar church that they would take the chairs down, so we set the chairs up, and they took them down. Well then I was saying, in my wildest dreams I never thought that several years later I could get a cocktail at the same place where I had received the sacraments in the schoolhouse. And it's now the Green Door.

Lucy Malmo: I do know that Reserve gave all the property for the churches in town. That they took the people out, and they looked at several places and decided where they would like to build their church, and they gave them the property. When we first moved, Sychar wasn't there.

Pat Lorntson: Another thing that Reserve did was, they said, "We will give three parcels of land, and you can choose, you know, and you can have a Protestant church, a Catholic church, and a Lutheran church."

Tim Bjella: I remember coming into Silver Bay and parking in front of the apartments. My wife and I were unloading stuff into the apartment, and a guy came running down the hill, and he said, "Are you the choir director here?" I said, "Yeah. We're starting this year." He says, "Well you're going to want to come to my church." He said, "We need a choir director." "Wait a minute!" Not even moved into the house, and they were recruiting people.

Evelyn Turonie: We had a temporary church in a Quonset hut. We went on a Sunday morning, and [the company's representative] said, "Come, put on your boots, and we'll go pick out sites. We'll show you what sites they have." They had four sites, and Sychar church is one of them, and they had picked that already. We had these other three sites to go to. I can't remember any one except this one as you come in town by the rock, the big rock, that was a site that was designated for church. I don't remember where the other two were. We picked our church because they said, "There's going to be a school right across the road from us." So it would be practical, if you had overflow, they could park at the school.

Helen Robinson*: When we first started going to church, we went to the Baptist Church that was in the Beaver Bay school, and then we built our own church on Highway 61, and we've been going there ever since. We started going to the Palisade Baptist Church in 1956.

Marie Frey*: I remember when Reserve Mining had their first open house. Up until that point, no one could get into Reserve Mining unless you worked there and had all the proper badges and identification. But they were having this open house, and we knew about it, as we would get a letter from Reserve about what was going to go on. They had asked the churches if they would serve coffee and donuts. All the churches wanted to do this, because there would be a check for our group, and we all needed money because we were starting out with our churches and we hardly had anything. All of the people wanted us to work. I go to Sychar Lutheran Church, and we were told by grapevine no, that's not the way Reserve did things. They had so many women work the morning shift from the Catholic Church, from the Lutheran Church, and I don't remember now if it was the Baptist or the U.P. Church, but it was three churches, and there were so many women from each church that worked the afternoon shift. We did this, I believe, for three or four days out of that week. That was Reserve's way of getting us together. I really think that's why we have such communication and affiliation with each other all through the years, to this day.

Ken Pellett: The company owned the clinic or dispensary. They had the first doctors, the first ambulance, and the first security, they had their own security force, and they bought all the equipment for the town here.

Matt Banovetz: The company built clinics and hired doctors to take care of the people. So, there's definitely advantages in this respect; however, when you look at the other side, people had very little to say about who manned the clinic and where the clinic was going to be built or anything else.

Marge Walentiny: There were a lot of babies that were born in Silver Bay, too, in the old clinic, and Vern helped with a lot of them.

Vern Walentiny: First of all, [when I worked at the clinic] I worked for Hunkin Arundel Dixon. And then [the plant] took us over, and then I started working for Reserve. "You got a new employer today," that's it.

We had an ambulance that we went to highway accidents. We went to practically anything that happened. I never took part in a rescue because Dr. Bloom wouldn't let me. I worked for the fire department for a few years, and I finally quit that, too.

Marge Walentiny: He did work on the rescue squad until Dr. Bloom asked him not to do that—none of the workers that were in the dispensary—because they needed them there most of the time.

Jenny Heinzen*: When the Rescue Squad was first forming, we were pretty proud. The VFW Auxiliary decided they wanted to do something to help the Rescue Squad get started, so somewhere in the material we got, we sent for this big poison antidote kit. We thought that might be handy as we were so far from the hospital and all. About a month later, we got a letter back from the rescue squad thanking us for the snake bite kit. The funny thing is, who's ever had a poisonous snake bite in this country?

Fran Jevning*: I worked for the city as policewoman for 28 years, and I retired from that. I've been on the Silver Bay Rescue and Ambulance for 13 years, and that's still going on. You wear a pager 24 hours a day, and when it goes off, you take off. We get pages from the Two Harbors dispatcher, and he tells us where the party is that needs help, and you report to the hall and meet the others there and go. We have a rescue unit and an ambulance unit, so that way the ambulance would not be paged out to a woods search. If they would find somebody that was hurt, then they would call out the ambulance. It kind of helps to have it divided that way. It's a wonderful privilege to work on it. I have enjoyed being able to help people. It's been a big part of our lives. Karl has it down to a science when I go out on a call. He knows the area and about how long it will take us, so he knows when I'll be back home.

George Starkovich: The medical facilities that we had were largely endorsed and/or supplemented and/or funded by the coffers of Reserve Mining Company when they were here. The original dispensary was located across the road from where the corner station is now, down by the stoplights. There was a dispensary there, and it was a company doctor. The company doctor saw everybody in the community.

Lucy Malmo: There was 24-hour coverage in the [dispensary/clinic]. They had these men—they were all men—that were sort of techs. Al Grosnick was an R.N., but they weren't all R.N.'s, but they had been trained. Some of them, I think Vern Walentiny had had service training in doing some lab work. Our kids were young, and we took them down there, but then Dr. Bloom had the building built where it is now. The thing is, how many places could you call the medical building at two o'clock in the morning and say, "Could you check my blood pressure?" The people on shifts would come down in the middle of the night, and there was somebody up in the building 24 hours. They'd run down anytime of the day or night to have a little thing checked or something. I think of Dr. Clifford, how he was there at six in the morning and at ten at night. Everyone was employed by the Reserve Mining, except the laboratory. I was an employee of the doctor who hired me, and the person that worked in the laboratory. We had a moderately complex laboratory; it wasn't just a physician's office lab. The doctors like laboratory work, and it was a full course of laboratory work.

There were those who took advantage of what was there. People would come in and sit down, call long distance, and use the phones. It wasn't a tight place; you could come in the back door and go through and that sort of thing. I think how simply it was run, but everything was kept track of. There was only a nurse or two and one person doing the book work and somebody in the lab and a few others, but they did so many things.

Wayne Johnson: Most of those doctors worked 18 hours a day or more.

Judy Kaiser: You never had to make an appointment. We would bring our kids there in the morning to see if we should send them off to school, and they'd check to see if they had a sore throat or if they had a fever. You could come day and night and be taken care of.

Helen Robinson*: If one of the kids got sick and I'd call him before 8 o'clock in the morning, [Dr. Haase would] come to the house and treat whoever was sick. We only had one car, and Malvin Robinson was working, so I couldn't get to the doctor's office, so he came to the house. He was a good guy.

Tootie LeBlanc: We were in home heating, which [my husband Pat's] dad had started up here, and now we purchased it from him later on. We did the business and the office work right in the house at 46 Davis Drive, until we moved to Highway 61 in 1969. And we've been there ever since.

Pat LeBlanc: The mine had their fuel truck, and they had people who delivered fuel around the plant. They don't do that anymore. They just assign you the contract, and you just take care of it. That's all they wanted, was it taken care of. Today my sons they take care of Babbitt and here. So it's a big, big commitment.

[Practically] nobody worked anyplace other than the mine. Of course, you had a few in the post office, and what may be, all that expanded like you wouldn't believe.

Arlene Pellett: They had a jewelry store here: Fortier Jewelers. That always blew my mind, because, in this small community, a jewelry store, because that's where [my husband] used to buy me a lot of my Christmas and birthday presents.

Ken Pellett: But they discouraged small business, because there wasn't any extra buildings to be had, unless somebody sold it out, there wasn't anything to be had.

Tootie LeBlanc: Because they were curtailed on building.

Ken Pellett: Galbreath owned that whole shopping mall. There was a hardware in the back corner there, and Malmo had a fountain service in the front.

Evie Buetow*: When they started the shopping center, we had more stores than we do now. Wally Fortier had a jewelry shop. We had Vertelny's clothing store. We had a shoe repair shop. We had the Malmo Drugstore, with its wonderful old-fashioned soda fountain. The day that they were forced to take that soda fountain out of that drugstore was a sad day. It was a foolish law or regulation that they had to remove this wonderful old fashioned soda fountain. That was a sad day.

Ruth Koepke: We had the grocery store, restaurant, a barber shop, a beauty shop, a jewelry store, a clothing store, the Malmo Drug, we had all these all along in a row. And the Minnesota Power, B.K. Hardware.

Tom Langley: Then one time we had a Montgomery Wards store. And a laundromat.

Bob Oslund: The barber shop with the three barbers. You go in the barber shop and they had like a lab coat on. They'd stand behind the chair and wait for you to make a choice.

Tootie LeBlanc: We had bowling, different companies sponsored different bowling competitions. I can't remember what year the bowling alley was built, but we had bowling teams, I don't know how many.

Ken Pellett: It was in the basement of the Union Hall. I'm sure the steelworkers paid for it.

Bob Oslund: The company had good things, lots of good things. Bowling, the top 12 from Silver Bay had to go up to Babbitt and bowl against the top 12 up there, and it was the same with golf. And they give good gifts.

Tootie LeBlanc: Then there was the curling club, and the chamber of commerce.

Ken Pellett: There was Lions Club, too. There was a Jaycees.

Evie Buetow*: We had a ski hill in Silver Bay right behind the second water tower, and it was a big deal. I'm not talking about the one up the highway. I'm talking about the one behind the town here. Behind the second water tower, they had a road back in there. That was a big thing! There was a groundbreaking ceremony and speech, and when it was all done we had a rope tow. Nancy Evenson [later, Mismash] was very instrumental in starting that. That didn't last too long, though. Roy Jacobson also worked on this. The Silver Bay Ski Hill was completed in 1956.

It was sponsored by the Lion's Club. Roy Jacobson did a lot of the leg work. It was located just north of Silver Bay.

Bob Oslund: There's still, up by the water tower, a block of cement. There was a tow rope where the kids that were skiing on that steep part of that hill didn't have to climb to the tower. And the block is still there from that.

Nancy Mismash: In fact, we had, we went on the road out to this place, and it was a chair lift. It had a rope tow, and I can remember giving skiing lessons to some of the people that would want to come out there.

Ruth Koepke: Now did the company put that up, pay for that?

Nancy Mismash: Mmhmm. Roy Jacobson got the people who made the road out there.

Tom Langley: When I was in junior high, we had this coach whose name was Mr. Smithback. He was my first football coach, my first basketball coach, and he heard that some of us were skiing out at the ski hill. He said, "I don't want any of you guys skiing. It's the best way you can turn your ankle or get hurt..." or whatever. Well, being kids, we didn't listen to that very much, so we were up there, and they had this competition. You could come roaring down, there's a little jump, and you can go maybe 20 feet. Well they had Mr. Smithback be the judge out there, and here I am coming down the hill, and he never said a word to me about, "Why are you out here?" He kind of gave me a funny look.

Donna Beaupre: And then the Bjork boys had the roller rink that they put out at the end of the shopping center, and you could rent skates.

Evie Buetow: Way back when I first started [teaching piano lessons], my goodness, I think I had about 20 students and was teaching piano lessons in our home. I mean, how much noise does that make or create for neighbors? I'm not going to mention names, because that's not proper, but somebody that was on the church council at the time decided that everybody that taught piano lessons should pay for and get a permit to do so. To teach piano lessons in your house! Well anyway, it was a long, drawn-out process. We had the pastor of a church, Inerson—his wife taught piano lessons—who was a very legal-minded man. He was sort of our legal advisor. It wasn't the money, it was the principle of the thing that I fought and fought and fought. I mean, it was $10. We went to meetings, and I wrote to piano teachers all over this part of the state. Nobody had ever heard of it before. So we had a certain date we were supposed to pay our $10 by, Friday at 4:00, and my husband kept saying, "Honey, just pay it. Just pay it, and be quiet. Just get it over with. Go down there with your $10." "No! I'm not going." So at noon on that Friday, guess who's at my door? The chief of police: Don Suess. And he had sort of a sheepish look on his face. Now I don't know where this would've led to, but he said, "You know what, Ev, you've gotta pay, you've gotta get that permit by four today. I came up to warn you that, if you don't, I'm going to have to issue you a warrant for your arrest." So it got to be later and later, and Harry would call from the office once in awhile, "Did you go? Did you go?" "No. No. No." So at one minute to four, I relented, went down there with my lousy ten bucks, and they were all waiting for me in there. Irritated me ever since.

Marie Frey*: When we first came here, there wasn't really many jobs, but there were very few babysitters. We didn't have teenagers in this town, and it was very hard to get a sitter, especially if you had to go to Duluth. I did a lot of babysitting in my home, because then I was home to take care of my own children.

Mary Carlson*: L.C. Hanson came and collected the garbage, threw the dog a bone—no dog laws then. They knew he was coming and they waited for the bone. He was good to them. Bill Loeffert was milkman. He plowed through the mud. He made sure everybody had milk, and I don't think he ever missed a time. He was a happy man. You knew he was coming; he was always whistling and always had a cheery word, and if you wanted to talk a minute, he took that minute. He was a good guy.

Wayne Johnson: I don't think people realize what Reserve contributed to the community. Even after we organized Silver Bay into a village at that time, they still were furnishing all kinds of equipment. If the street department didn't have something, literally within minutes there'd be a Reserve piece of equipment there.

Pat LeBlanc: You know, when we lived way up here, we didn't have access to everything. And if I ever needed a motor to load trucks, I called down there, and they'd send a guy out with a new motor—not necessarily a new one, but one that would work. All I had to do when I got one, I just had to bring it back, that was the only restriction.

Tootie LeBlanc: Anytime we needed a tank or something, they were right over there to move it and put it in place.

Ken Pellett: Even after we opened our machine shop—of course I knew some of the right people to ask—when I needed a cherry picker crane, we got a big machine in, and they came right out and set it for me.

Pat LeBlanc: And no charge.

Ken Pellett: They furnished the city with dump trucks and 'dozers and graders and the buildings to store all this. And fire trucks and rescue squads.

Clarence Roeben: I know when we needed a new fire truck, all we had to do was ask, and I saw the checks written. Reserve Mining Company covered it; it was very nice. A lot of blessings here. The police car, for example. If we needed a street sweeper, or anything to do with fire protection, they were right there. Back in the days, Reserve had their own fire department before the city incorporated.

Jim Gordon: Everyone knew if you had an emergency or needed to get in touch with your spouse working in the plant—day or night—you just had to call the main gate at Reserve. No need to call 911 for the sheriff; the main gate had immediate contact with the sheriff, as well as the volunteer fire department.

Marie Frey*: I remember that I worked at an organization and I had to do some typing, and there was no way to buy this paper here, and I knew who to speak to and went right over and got a ream of paper. The Girl Scouts, we started up and we didn't have anything—not even a meeting place. Finally we found that we could meet in someone's home in the basement, but there weren't any chairs or tables. Reserve Mining sent over tables and chairs. If we needed it, we could go to Reserve, and when we asked, "Who do we send a letter of thanks to?" The reply was: "There is no one to thank, just go ahead; if you need something else, just come to us." They never wanted any thank you, and they did so many things for this town. Things that people don't even realize that we depended so much on them.

Ken Pellett: Another thing: People here were real fortunate if you enjoyed golfing. You could golf at a real reasonable price compared to other clubs around the country. But if there was a sneeze or a wheeze at the country club, when I was yards and docks, we had two supervisors that said, "Get the pickup. We're going to the country club. We got trouble."

George Starkovich: When the big steel strike came, the plant shut down for awhile. During that time period, that's when the golf course began to be built. All of the salaried workers, the people who were supervisors that were not members of the local steelworkers union were kept on staff, and they worked out at the country club, clearing the country club and seeding the fairways and this, that, and the other thing. So the country club became again a place where folks could go out and enjoy the game of golf. It was also a place of some stature. It's located on the former Betzler homestead.

I recall when we first moved here going out before anything was out there. There was a partial barn standing there. As a matter of fact, I've got some horseshoes that I found out there. But my dad and I went out, and there was this beautiful piece of the Beaver River flowing through one of the lower pastures. It was just so serene. Where the clubhouse stands right now was part and parcel of land where the homestead and the barn were. What a beautiful area that was. I thought, I'll never forget how pastoral that place looked, and it still is a beautiful area.

They did a nice job of putting in the golf course. As a child growing up there, there certainly seemed to me to be kind of a caste system in a way in terms of the golf course. I was fortunate enough to secure a job out there—a summer job when I was a student in high school. Most of the people that played golf at that time were the upper echelon of the people that worked in the plant. I don't know if you had to be invited to be a member of the country club or not. I never asked the question, because back when I was there in the '50s, you didn't ask questions, you just did what you were told to do. Just from the people that were there, it appeared to me that you had to be of a certain social status to be able to participate in the activities that were present out there. I do recall that most of the department heads were members of the country club, and I do recall that some upper echelon school administrators were also out there. Whether or not they were members, I don't know. It was definitely a great experience for me to work out there. I felt privileged that I had the job.

Whether it was fact or fancy in my head, I don't know, but it always appeared to me that the top leaders and top administrators in the company or the managers always held a very respected spot in the country club. There was one area of the main room in the corner that was always reserved for those individuals. I was told, I didn't ever witness it because I never went to any social events out there, but I was told that there was a dance out there, a Christmas dance or something, that nobody danced until the head of the company or the people that were sitting at the corner table got up to dance. Then everybody else was able to join in.

Mickey Lorntson: The company spent a lot of money keeping up [the country club]. We had this procedure where if you had to do something at the golf course, they didn't have a charge account for it. This was all getting buried in something else. The concentrator'd take a hit one day on work that was being done there. The company did a lot of work there—you know, fit it under the table. It never got published in the specs.

Maggie King: But everybody knew, and it was a country club with the aura of an echeloning, definitely, of people who could go.

Dick King: Well, first only the staff members could use it, like foremen on up. They had teachers, and finally everybody. Whenever there was a strike or a slowdown, then all the staff members would go work there, building the little sheds.

Lucy Malmo: We were members of the club in the beginning.

Tom Malmo: I used to be a salesman out there. I sold the golf carts.

Wayne Johnson: We were members, and there were a lot of guys from that plant that were workers in the plant that were members.

Evelyn Turonie: I had golfed a little bit when I was living in Milwaukee, and I was interested in the golf course, and I called up Mr. Cooksey and asked him if there were certain specific things you have to do to be a member. He said, "Yeah, pay." And I called him about 10:00 in the morning, and before noon there was a rap on the door—it was Mr. Cooksey, and he said, "If you want to be a member, I'll take your money right now." That same day, he took our money, and everybody else around had said it was private—you couldn't afford that. That's how fast we got in.

I wouldn't say that they treated me different, but we were the second hourly wages person that had joined this club. The other thing I remember was, when you went out there in the evening, like on a Saturday night, men had to have jackets—a suit and tie.

Clarence Roeben: I enjoyed the country club because every one of our kids got an opportunity to play. It wasn't my piece of cake, but I didn't hamper because it was a good recreation place. If anything had to be done on the buildings out there, I got an opportunity to put my two hands on it, so I helped them in many different ways.

Lucy Malmo: Yeah, I think a lot of the workers took advantage of having the golf course here. Maybe if they'd been somewhere else they wouldn't have been playing golf.

Chuck Kaiser: Jim Reynolds, one of my favorite people, had a droll sense of humor, and he was not afraid to take shots at the very people that were his compatriots down there in management and stuff like that. The first president, Jim said, had his table—over to the right, in the back of the clubhouse, the big round table. And right down on the wall just by the table there was a button, and Jim says people would come there, and they'd sit around this table to eat, and they couldn't figure out how every time, these waitresses would pop out just at the precise moment when something was needed—the president needed a refill of his drink, or something like that—but he had this button back there that he'd press, and when he'd press it, they'd come running. Jim was part of the group, so he knew it. I've seen the buzzer, but I didn't know what it was until he told me.

Tim Bjella: I don't know if other teachers felt this way: When we were first there, teachers were not discouraged from going to the country club, but were not appreciated much, because it really was management that used it.

Maggie King: It was very private.

Chuck Kaiser: Even after it was opened up and I became a member, because of Dick Lynch, there were certain individuals, who will go unnamed, who had a very terrible attitude about us infringing on their territory out there. We didn't really belong there, and they made it pretty clear.

Pat LeBlanc: You used to buy two steak dinners out there for $7 for two people, and that would've been $15 anyplace else.

Tootie LeBlanc: Yeah, everything was pretty much half price.

Irene Johnson*: When they first opened up, I was waitress, barmaid, I did the dishes and the salads. I did cook, too, sometimes, but like on a Friday or Saturday night, it was Walt Morrison and myself out there. He did the cooking, and I did everything else. A lot of nights I had to call [my husband] Willy to come and help wash dishes, because we had no dishwasher, and I wouldn't get out of there until three in the morning and have to be back in at eight or nine in the morning to start up again. Then I'd cook the short orders and take care of everything at that time. One night we served 75 people, I believe it was, Walt and myself, and I got $20 in tips, and I thought I had the world by the tail.

Evie Buetow: In the very beginning, if you didn't have a membership, you could not go out there for dinner.

Ed Hynes: A membership was about $75 a year.

Evie Buetow: That was a big deal, you know, way back then. That was a higher part of this whole system, too, until the day came when they allowed people to go out there for dinner.

Lois Hynes: And for lunch.

Evie Buetow: But then, you had to be careful what table you sat at, because there were certain tables—round tables.

Lois Hynes: The round table in the corner.

Evie Buetow: Remember that? And you don't sit there!

Ed Hynes: Being in purchasing, I'd go out there for lunch with salesmen from time to time. And it was always an excellent lunch. Part of my job was going to lunch with salesmen.

Lois Hynes: I know we used to go out there for Saturday night dinners and sit out on the porch, and in the winter when the snow would come down on those big trees.

Evie Buetow: It was so beautiful.

Lois Hynes: You know, you just felt like you were in the lap of luxury.

Ed Hynes: There was one time my mother was up, and the whole Hynes tribe was there, and we sat at that big round table in the corner.

Bob Eckstrom: That was for the elite in the beginning. But that changed. It was a beautiful course, still is.

Betty Oslund: But that's very true, it was considered an elite symbol, and it was really something, if you weren't in that group to be able to go out there.

Bob Eckstrom: The bigwigs, they'd sit out there at the golf course part of the day. You'd go out there and do some work. Something would go wrong down at the golf course, and you had to go out there and fix something.

Art Przybilla: They sometimes ran people from the labor pool to do jobs on the golf course. As a matter of fact, I can remember that summer that I was in the labor pool, we pulled garbage out of there, and then we went and cleaned under a bridge one time.

Nancy Mismash: Whenever the strike was on, they worked out there.

Ruth Koepke: And plant protection had to go out every night and help them close and [deal with the] money.

Anne Przybilla: I remember one year the faculty Christmas party was held at the country club, and that was really a big deal, because most of us had never been there.

Ruth Koepke: The company had also built a big auditorium so that a lot of events were held there, and they didn't have to pay rent for it. They had all the New Year's Eve parties and all that stuff down there.

Irene Johnson*: I worked at the commissary and did a lot of parties for "big wheels." I also worked at the country club. I went on the train to Babbitt; I served a meal there with Walter Morrison. He and I served on the way up, and neither one of us knew how to walk on the train, much less serve on a train. President Linney was there at the time, and he showed me how to stand and pour a cup of coffee. Walt Morrison was in charge of [the commissary]. A head chef at that time. They were open, when I worked there, from five in the morning 'til ten at night, I believe. When I first started there, it was the only [restaurant]. There was lots of dances. We had two different side rooms where you could have two different things going on at one time. Lots of style shows, banquets, and stuff like that was at the commissary.

Willis Johnson*: That was the meeting place. Or the Union Hall.

Jim Gordon: Weddings, anniversaries, dinners, pancake breakfasts, dances, union meetings: The Union Hall could handle it all. The dances at the Union Hall were the best. There were always great bands and the ladies presented a grand lunch at the end of the evening. Everyone came to dance the night away.

Bob Eckstrom: But if we didn't have the plant here, we wouldn't have had any of this. The plant was why Silver Bay's here.

Mary Carlson*: Reserve was very good to us. They were like parents to all of us that worked for them. I think they were almost too good to us.

CHAPTER 5

SCHOOLS

Reserve Mining Company built three state-of-the-art schools in Silver Bay. The high school included facilities and equipment more commonly seen in colleges than at lower educational levels. The value that company executives placed on education was clear in the partnership that the company had with the schools. Students were imbued with an uncommon education ethic that practically compelled them to pursue higher education. Even further, Silver Bay kids seemed genetically programmed to go out into the world and make something of themselves—to be pioneers, as their parents had been.

Tim Bjella: Now, the first school was Campton, the elementary school. It was a beautiful school, as you can see what's left of it. After that was used, they built the high school. And Mary Mac [MacDonald] School didn't come around until [later].

Pat Lorntson: They were brand new. The facilities were brand new.

Tim Bjella: And the mining company helped a lot.

Nancy Mismash: When I started teaching, Campton had just started, and our gradebooks looked like we didn't know how to organize anything, because there were kids coming and going constantly with the construction people. Sometimes I had 45 in a class, and sometimes maybe 40 or something, and it was changing all the time, and we were crossing out and adding and that sort of thing. I taught phy ed, and the girls were in one class and the boys in another. Right above the gym was the projection room, and that's where Merlin Moore had shop. We'd be in a class, and all of a sudden, "Hey, look at what they're doing," and there the boys would be peeking out the hole and watching the girls in their phy ed. We had a little thing going. My office at Campton was right next to the general office, and that was Mr. Granger's office. And Mr. Granger is the one that wrote our school song, and he would be writing it, and he'd come in and say, "How do you think this sounds?" And then we'd go over it, and we'd do it, and then he'd do some more, and we worked it over. It was fun to realize that he did the school song, and it's still here.

Tom Langley: About the Campton gym and that little projection booth: We were up there one day, and I guess Mr. Moore was my homeroom teacher, if we had homeroom in those days. But they came out, and they said we have to give the school a nickname, and there was like five names on the board. Pellets was one of them that I remember, Bruins and Bears and Polar Bears, and there was one I don't know. Well, anyway, this [one] guy was very good at art. He was a year ahead of me, but he never graduated, and he moved away. Well anyway, he drew a beautiful polar bear in a circle, and he also did the logo, and then those names came up there, and Polar Bear was one. We were the Silver Bay Polar Bears. Well, we found out that we were in the same league as Floodwood, which was the Polar Bears. We could not take Polar Bears, so they said. "Okay, we've gotta do it all over again. If anybody has any ideas, tomorrow morning we're going to throw names in a hat, and somebody will pick five of them and put them up there." So I was at home, and I was watching *The Arthur Godfrey Show,* and they had a vocal group on there called The Mariners. It was an [integrated group of white and] African-American [Coast Guard veterans] called The Mariners. I looked at that, and I thought, "Geez, that might not be a bad name." We had boats coming in here to take away our pellets, and coal coming in here, and so on and so forth. So I threw "Mariners" in the hat the next day. Five more names. Pellets were back up there, Silver Bay Pellets. Well, I was told that Mariners won hands-down—they really, really liked the name. I got two dollars and fifty cents for naming them the Mariners.

Nancy Mismash: That must've been before Bob Granger started making up his song. "We are the North Shore Mariners," and so on.

Tom Langley: Oh yeah, it had to be. He had to make up the song after that. That was a very interesting thing, and I'm glad it's going to be in some kind of a record. Some people knew that I had named it, and they ask me how the story went, but that's as good as I can remember it.

Dick King: Back at Campton, and all the different things going on in one place at once. I think it was the second year I was there, I went to visit with Dave Schnorr, who was doing woodshop in the projection booth. There were no fans; they had the windows open. There were kids going out picking agates on the rocks, on top. You'd look out, and there was a basketball court, and on the far end was a stage. Dave Schnorr's got his power equipment going, whirrrrrr, and then out here, Nancy Evenson [later, Mismash], who had the girls phy ed, and Claire Smithback had the boys phy ed on the other side, and Edgar Baseman had his whole band on the top.

Pat Lorntson: When Mary Mac was built, you know how it goes down at one place? Before they got that first part built, they had to put an addition on, and that's why you go down [a half-level at one end]. They just didn't plan big enough, and we just had too many kids.

Marjorie Jorgenson*: Not long after school got started, there were so many kindergartners that for a time there were three "shifts" of kindergartners—morning, noon, and afternoon classes.

Dick King: [We moved into the permanent high school building in] 1958. Right after school got over, we got all the teachers and custodians. We got our pickups and trucks and whatnot, and we hauled stuff out to Kelley from there.

George Starkovich: After the high school was built, the first class to graduate was 1959. The school was a model of school buildings, a model of architecture, a model of sustainability, the types of materials that were used in the building. The building is as sound today as it was the day it was built. The only thing that has suffered from the ravages of nature is a bit of spalling on some of the brick walls, which have been replaced, and the roofs, of course, which have to be replaced.

I had an extremely unique opportunity. I graduated there in 1961, and I went to college and began teaching down in St. Francis. I was drafted in the military, got out of Vietnam in 1969, came back and started to work in the school district. I didn't ever plan to have it this way. In fact, I never even planned to be a teacher, but as fortune and destiny proceeded down the line, I became the principal of William

Kelley High School, the very school that I graduated from. To demonstrate the professionalism of the teachers and the educational staff that I had the good fortune to receive my education from, I was named principal while at the same time a good many of those teachers were still teaching. Imagine being a teacher, and here comes one of your former students who you had taught in high school. He has been named the principal of your high school, and now he is in a position of being your supervisor. Not one of those teachers—and there were probably six to ten teachers left—ever made any derisive comments about being a former student or anything else. To me that marks the professionalism of the staff that we had here and still do.

The teachers that came in to teach were overwhelmed by the school. Reserve Mining Company built the entire school. It didn't cost the school district anything. I served on several building committees while I was administrator here in the district, and we recently, four years ago, spent about $34 million to build a new high school in Two Harbors, and the sustainability of that building nowhere compares to the sustainability of the high school that our students still attend here in Silver Bay which was built in 1957. To rebuild the building that we have now would probably cost in excess of $50 million.

There was such a partnership between the school system and Reserve Mining Company—it was unbelievable. For instance, the big light poles that we have. Our first football field was at Campton [School]. We played on an 80-yard field down there, because it wasn't long enough. We didn't have a football field. Even when the high school was first built, the football field wasn't done, so we still played football down on the 80-yard field. When they finally built the football field, they had these great big towers. Tom Malmo used to climb those towers and film with his wind-up camera. Those towers waved back and forth, but he'd be up there. Tom was a legend in his own time. Everybody just loved him—the kids loved him. He would shoot off fireworks, which were kind of contraband in those days. Every time Silver Bay scored, he'd light some kind of fireworks and shoot 'em off of the towers.

Sometimes, if we had to change a light bulb or something, the school didn't have the equipment, so they could call down to the plant, and they'd send up the electrical department with a basket that had the extension arm on it to change the lights. If we needed something big that had to be lifted or something, they'd send up a cherry picker.

When I was principal at the school, for welding classes we were going through lots of steel, and I'd call down there and say, "Hey, you know, we need a skiff of scrap steel." And here they'd come with a big truck, a service truck with a skiff of steel on it, that would be followed by a cherry picker, and a truck helper would get out and hook up the skiff of steel to the cherry picker. The cherry picker would pick it up and deposit the steel next to the metal shop and pick up the old skiff that we had emptied out, used for projects. Then they'd head on their merry way.

Reserve Mining Company was a benefactor to this community from the word "go." You talk about corporate responsibility, how some corporations now just utilize their people and throw them away and things of that sort. Reserve Mining

Company took care of its own. I mean, look at the schools that they built. They said, "Hey, we want a good place for our kids to be able to go to school."

To tell you, for example, when our school was built, Mr. Bryant was one of the guys who was in charge of the monetary dealings of Reserve Mining Company. He stipulated that he wanted a nine-foot grand piano—a Steinway—installed in the school when the school was built. He stipulated to the architects that a special room would be built for that piano. So a special room was built for that piano. It had a thermostatic control in it to monitor the humidity and everything, and that piano is the same piano that is there today. Now the worth of that piano is astronomical, even today. I have a cousin who is in the music business, and he does piano restoration. He would give his eyeteeth, his left arm, and several fingers to get his hands on that nine-foot grand. I told him when I was principal, I said, "We've got a nine-foot grand." He says, "No you don't." I said, "We do, too." He said, "I'll tell you what. When you get back to the Bay, one day when you have an opportunity, you go down there and you take the number off of that piano." I said, "Where is it?" He said, "Open it up on the sound board, and there's this plate." And he said, "You said it's a Steinway, right?" He said, "No no, there's no way that you have a nine-foot Steinway in your school." So I called him back, I said, "Here's the number." And then it was silent on the other end of the phone. I said, "Rod, are you there?" He says, "Yeah." He said, "You *do* have a nine-foot Steinway there." He gave me the history of it, where it was manufactured, and so on. He said, "Would the school district be willing to sell it?" At that time he was telling me that the piano itself, before any kind of restoration and stuff, was worth at least $40 to $50 thousand. So I don't know how much it's worth, but that's the kind of thinking that went into the building of that place.

Evie Buetow: I was really happy when they got the grand piano. [Our son] David was a very fine pianist. He went into music in college. He played with the orchestra *Rhapsody in Blue* one year, and Doc Davis was there, and he just got up, practically started a standing ovation, and he was a pioneer. He'd champion everything in our town. It's a beautiful piano, and it keeps tune very, very well.

Lois Hynes: Tim Bjella gave [our son] Mike the key one summer and he said, "Anytime you want to go in there and practice, you go ahead." He says, "It's good for the piano, and it's good for you."

Ed Hynes: Oh, it was just a fantastic piano.

Pat Lorntson: A few years ago when finances were kind of tough, George Starkovich wanted to sell the piano. Oh boy, he would've had a bunch of angry people on his back. Oh, I'll tell you. They would've skun him alive, because you don't touch that piano. There was a Northern Lake County Arts Board that I'm a member of, and we raised money to have it all redone.

Art Przybilla: In 1968, I worked for Mike Tourje at the plant for one summer when I was in industrial engineering, half a summer. I met him someplace, I don't remember where, but he said, "You know what you need over at that school?" I said, "What's that?" And he said, "You need one of these new videotape recorders." And I said, "Yeah, well I'm sure we could use one in speech class and things of that sort."

He said, "You would use it, huh?" I said, "Yeah." He says, "Put in for one." And I said, "Um, okay." I went and looked at a couple of them at an MEA convention down in Minneapolis, and I went to [Principal] Frank Rukavina and said, "I'd like to have a videotape recorder for my speech class." He laughed a little bit. About three days later, he called me down and he said, "I think we're going to get that videotape recorder." Of course, I found out years later that it was Mike Tourje that had said, "Get this particular gear." As I understand it, Reserve Mining gave a little money to the school or something, and we had the first videotape recorder in any high school in the state. After we got it, and we were using it a little while, all of a sudden, I open my classroom door one morning, and there were two giant metal boxes, and they had video cameras inside. They had just taken down the cameras up that were overlooking the yards down at the plant, and they replaced them, and they gave us the old ones. They gave us all sorts of things.

We made rocks one time for a play. They had just put in all sorts of foam insulating the bridge, the pellet bridge. They had sprayed it in, and when they sprayed it in, they had gone to where it would drip off, it would form piles, and they looked like rocks. The next play that we did had big styrofoam rocks.

George Starkovich: Probably the only mistake that was made in building the theatre department was, the fly space above the stage wasn't tall enough. It could've been another 10 or 15 feet taller. But there was nobody within a 100-mile radius that had an auditorium like that, with all the up-to-date equipment and everything else. The quality of education that Reserve management wanted for its students was top priority. They walked hand-in-hand with us all the time, even when I was principal. I took over as principal in 1982. I'd worked for the school district since 1969. The support that we got from Reserve Mining Company was phenomenal.

Anne Przybilla: We came to the North Shore on our honeymoon and stopped to see a good friend of ours, and he took us on a tour of the school. I can remember going through the school and just gasping and saying, "Oh, can you imagine teaching in a building like this. Can you imagine?"

Betty Oslund: I think they wanted state-of-the-art schools, and the facilities that they had here, for their workers' children.

Chuck Kaiser: When we came here, we were told that since Reserve Mining had come into the school district, there had never been a levy. Reserve simply built the buildings, and then they just deducted it from their tax liability for the next couple of years.

Pat Lorntson: The company did build all of these schools, and there never was a bond issue—never.

Matt Banovetz: My wife used to say that the science department—her major was science—was equipped as good, or better than, a college, and she went to St. Olaf. The company, through the Reserve scholarship, recognized students for outstanding work. It was good to see, even though at the end I never could get them to increase the value of the scholarship as the price of going to school increased.

Judy Kaiser: One reason we came here was because of the schools. Everything was relatively new, and the pay up here for teachers was twice what we were making in Grand Rapids, Minnesota. We came in, and they did everything. I remember when they gave us a tour of the building, they had a grand piano, and Reserve Mining had put that in there.

Lucy Malmo: Everything was new, and everything they asked for, they got. The teachers were young, and they were enthusiastic, and everything was just wonderful because of the programs and the whole curriculum and everything to work with. They had everything, it was just a wonderful place.

Tim Bjella: When I came here, it was the first year the auditorium was finished. They spared no extra, I mean no limit to what was put into the buildings. We got, for example, a Steinway grand piano, which is still there and a top-notch piece of equipment. I think we had musical instruments that they bought, and they were all set up and ready. Most teachers would die to go to a school that had that kind of a facility. The high school was and still is one of the better looking schools.

Chuck Kaiser: When we came here, the first thing, Frank Rukavina gave me the grand tour. Their big thing was the pool, because I came from Grand Rapids, I taught there for five years, and they didn't have a pool. Then the auditorium, because that was spectacular compared to practically anyplace else you go. But then there's the school itself, because most schools, like Grand Rapids, had nice schools, and they had walls that were plaster, but here you had the wainscot with the tile on top of it. I mean, that's pretty decent stuff.

Maggie King: The materials of the building, the tile and the marble floors. The choir room and the band room were built in the semi-amphitheater layout and design like college.

Chuck Kaiser: They were building [the arena] when we came here. That's kind of interesting, too, because basically they built arenas here in Two Harbors because they had money, and the state had pretty much said, "Spend it or lose it," so they built two arenas. I think Hibbing was the only other school up here that had an arena. Anybody else that was playing hockey, they were using some other facility that didn't belong to the actual school district. When we came here, that was the first thing, as you come up Outer Drive, there's this great big arena being built.

Tim Bjella: I remember the first year or two that I was here, I had friends that were teachers that were coming from other schools and looking and being amazed at the condition of the looks of the school. And they said, "You know, five or ten years, and it's not going to look like this anymore," but it did.

Chuck Kaiser: It did. For 30 years, it did.

Tim Bjella: It looked almost, when I retired, the same as it did when I started.

Chuck Kaiser: The community took a lot of pride in the buildings. The custodians took a lot of pride, especially at the high school here.

Tim Bjella: I was going to mention, too, that when I first started, they wanted to know how much money I thought I needed to run my music department, and I didn't know, that was my second year teaching. And so they said, "How about $1,200?" We bought risers for the stage, we bought gowns, choir robes, and whatever we could think of. We bought books. I was thinking, when I retired, my budget was half of what it was when I started. These people knew what they needed. These guys were very well educated in theatre and so forth, so they bought good equipment and the right equipment.

Chuck Kaiser: Money was never an object. At least at the beginning, that was so clear when you saw how those rooms were furnished and so forth. One of the things that struck me, because I came from Grand Rapids, and the reason I left Grand Rapids was I'd taught there five years, and every year that I stayed there after that, I would've lost hundreds of dollars on the salary schedule compared to here. When we came here in '66, I got an $800-a-year raise because I was on the sixth step over what I would've gotten in Grand Rapids. Eight hundred dollars. That's pocket change today, but at that time, that was big. Then, to top it all off, we got started with the school year, and the school board had its first meeting, and they found out they had a little extra money, and they gave everybody in the whole district a $100 raise. Nobody even asked for it, so I thought I'd gone to heaven. At that time, the school board had kind of an unwritten rule that they had the top-ten-paying school districts of the state of Minnesota. And we had to be in the top ten, and usually toward the top of the top ten.

Bob Oslund: When I first came to the school, the beautiful school, I was interviewed by Bob Granger, and it was a Saturday afternoon. I went into his office, and he had his feet up on a big leather cushion. I said, "What if I want get one of those?" Well, I found out later he was doing it for health reasons. He'd had surgery; he needed to have his feet elevated. When I saw that leather cushion, I went, "Whew! Where do I sign?"

Chuck Kaiser: It seemed to me that here there was a high value placed on your education, and I always felt like we got a lot of support from parents here over the years, and that made teaching a lot easier because of that. And that was because they did value it so highly.

Pat Lorntson: When we had PTA meetings, and we sat in the gymnasium of Campton School, it was packed. It was just packed because education was so important.

Bob Oslund: At that time, when I met with parents, without exception, both parents said in our conference, "Let us know if there's anything we can do. We want our son or daughter to finish school, and if they can, go on to college." We had parent conferences, we had about 80 percent, 70 percent of parents in the high school show up. That was extraordinary.

Pat Lorntson: Our oldest boy graduated in '67 and the next one in '68, and the teaching then was fabulous. When they went off to college, we would hear things [from the colleges] like, "We love to have your kids coming in; they know how to write, they know how to study, they know how to learn." It was due to the teaching staff. It was a good, good teaching staff.

Tim Bjella: I never noticed that we were second to any other school. I remember the music department and the phy ed department and the theatre, which is what I worked in mostly, were always competitive or leading the way—every teacher will say with some reservation that the students we had then, probably the first ten years—were probably the better students that we had.

Chuck Kaiser: When we got here, there was a high percentage of students in every class whose parents were in management down at the plant. They were in one of those upper-level positions down there. Most people really emphasized education and supported it. It was pretty much that way among the rank-and-file workers, too, because they saw it as a way to get out of that. The largest number of kids in that building was about 980 and change in 1981, '82.

Tim Bjella: We could have an assembly of all those students, and they didn't break any seats, they didn't make much noise.

Pat Lorntson: They were proud of the school. They were really well behaved.

George Starkovich: A friend of mine whose son worked in Japan told me that, in Japan, if the kid gets in trouble in school, they would call the company that the child's father worked for, and the Japanese father would then be threatened by the company officials and say, "Hey, you'd better straighten your kid up, or you're going to wear this badge of shame" or whatever. Here in Silver Bay, you didn't have to do that because it was pretty open. If a kid got in trouble in school from a teacher, when he got home, he got in more trouble.

Ken Pellett: They pretty much got anything they wanted in these new schools—buses and everything. They had pretty much top-of-the-line everything. They had to, because they hauled students from as far away as Forest Center and clear down to the Gooseberry Bridge.

Evie Buetow: The education our kids got at that time was the best you could ever imagine. The school system, well there was a lot of help from Reserve building. They had everything.

Ed Hynes: You couldn't have a better school.

Evelyn Turonie: Even for the recreation, I don't know what part of Reserve did it, but our son was in the first grade when he came here, and the next summer he was on a team and he got a uniform. They bought uniforms for every little kid and sponsored all the athletic things possible.

Evie Buetow: It was a different feeling, the different camaraderie with so many after-school activities, too. The theatre department is one great big one that I remember because my kids were so involved in that. Look what they did. They went to state, winning award after award.

Rose Elam: I thought it was wonderful. My kids absolutely loved it. You know, they grow up and they think, "If I could just go someplace where there's more excitement and more things to do," but you should hear them talk now, how wonderful it was. There was always something to do. There was jobs for them to do in the summertime, and the sports that they participated in they just loved it.

Anne Przybilla: I think the school was really the heart of the community. This was a new place. There wasn't a movie theatre, there wasn't anything else, so the activities were all centered in the school. And everybody went to all of those activities.

George Pope: All the schools in the whole town were new. I was 12 or 13 when we moved to Silver Bay, the high school was being built, and we would be in a classroom, and next door they were building the classroom that we were gonna occupy the next year. So it's sort of unfolding in front of our eyes. And of course, what I'm saying is the high school was brand new. The swimming pool was brand new—we had a swimming team. We had all the athletics, including football, basketball, and baseball. In those days the girls didn't participate in organized athletics. My recollection, or what I've been told, is Reserve paid for everything, including our football team uniforms and band uniforms and the instruments.

George Starkovich: If something had to be done in the community, Reserve was there. There was never any doubt about it. One time it was thought that all the student athletes should have blue blazers with an anchor on them. Guess who bought them: Reserve Mining Company. Everybody that played football, basketball, everything. They had a company come in from Duluth and measure all the athletes. At the time there weren't any female teams. But all us guys got a blue blazer from Reserve Mining Company. The funny thing about it was that the school board had some difficulty early on accepting the generosity of Reserve because they felt that if Silver Bay got it, Two Harbors should get it, so then it got messy after several years. "Well, we can't accept that from Reserve Mining Company unless Two Harbors gets the same."

I believe that Reserve was a fantastic benefactor in this community. People were able to rest assured that if something was going on in the community, Reserve Mining would help out with it. I mean, if you needed steel to build uprights for the bleachers, who was there? Reserve Mining Company. If you needed help to erect the goalposts, who was there? Reserve Mining Company.

One unique thing that should be mentioned in any history of this community is the William Kelley family. Mr. William M. Kelley, who the high school is named after, worked as a common laborer in some of the steel mills out east, and he worked his way up through all the ranks and eventually became respected enough in the corporate field to be given the responsibility of running Reserve Mining Company as the president. He came to Silver Bay, and he oversaw the operation here, and there is a scholarship given to this day in honor of Mr. Kelley, and his family continues on a yearly basis to fund that scholarship. What a legacy. His portrait is in the foyer of the auditorium of the school, and rightly so, because his family has been responsible for many, many students receiving great assistance with their college educations.

Bob Oslund: There were scholarships from various groups, and then there was a union scholarship—there was to be no teacher evaluation there. There was also a tech scholarship. And then there was a Reserve scholarship. I went down and looked at IQ scores of all the classes we had, and there was no difference. It didn't make any difference where you came from, the brain kids came from everywhere. There was a cross-section right through, whether you're management, or whether your parents hadn't had an actual education, you were very bright.

Art Przybilla: If you were going to go to college, you could get summer employment. All you had to do was talk to Jim Andrews [in human resources]. If you talked to Jim before summer came around, they would have a spot for you to work down there, and it wasn't only the people that had graduated.

Tom Langley: I worked at the plant.

Art Przybilla: Teachers, too. I was on the labor pool. Teachers could go down there, if you talked to Jim Andrews. With teachers they made a little different deal: They wouldn't let you have a job down there in the summertime unless you agreed not to join the union. In order to do that, they would let you work only half the summer, like in the labor pool or driving a truck or something of that sort. Then, the other half of the summer, you had to be working in some sort of a management type of position.

Anne Przybilla: That was because after 30 shifts, you automatically were expected to join the union, so at the end of 30 shifts, teachers went to R&D or something, but it was a non-union position then.

Art Przybilla: Usually it was a job that you didn't know a thing about.

Tom Langley: I graduated in 1960, and I wasn't 18 until the middle of June. And my dad and I were talking; I was really down in the dumps. I said, "All the other kids are going to get a jump on me." He said, "Don't worry about it." So finally I went down to see Jim Andrews, and I got on, and for graduation I got a new suit—black suit—and a really nice wristwatch. Well, from the labor pool I got sent down to the concentrator, and we were digging with jackhammers—they were putting some sort of metal across there anyway for the laundry chute to go out. So we were tied down in harnesses, and I thought, "Oh boy, my watch, my new watch, I don't want to get jiggled," so I put it in the pocket of my shirt. And then I went down with the jackhammer and jackhammered away against my chest, and it came up and it took my watch. I can still see it this very day in slow motion, my brand new watch going right down, and in about two seconds it was gone. It's out in the metal ledge up there somewhere, as we speak. Working those summers, that was the greatest thing—got me through college. It was like a scholarship, then, but I did work really hard. $625 bucks that summer. I never spent one red cent on anything, and it still got me through my next year at college. $91 a quarter, that's what the tuition was at UMD in those days, in 1960, '61. And then the second year, when I was a sophomore in college, the plant didn't have anybody because of a strike, so I worked at the high school.

Bob Eckstrom: My older son and daughter worked down there, and it helped put them through college. When the plant first started, with all the problems they had, you could work 12 hours a day, 16 hours a day.

George Starkovich: I can remember, because I was a union member, and as a kid I had the good fortune to be able to work down at Reserve Mining Company in the summer. That was another way they helped out. It was automatic. Here's the scenario: You get done with graduation, you walk off the stage, the principal of the high school, Mr. Frank Rukavina, says, "I want to see everybody, I want to see all the boys." It was just boys at the time. "I want to see all of you guys downstairs in the cafeteria." We go downstairs, and he says, "Alright, all of you report to Reserve Mining Company tomorrow at 6:30 a.m. Anybody who wants to have a job at Reserve Mining Company for the summer, you go down there." You didn't have to have any certain grades or anything, you just went down there. We went down there, and they filed us all into one big room, and they said, "Okay, anybody that wants to work for the summer, fill out this application. Okay, here are the rules. You're hired for the summer. You're all going to be working job class two." That was the laborer. And in 1961, those of us that signed on the dotted line as job class-two laborers earned the mighty sum of $2.18 an hour.

The job classes went from, two was the laborer, the highest job class, I think, was job class 14 or 16, and that was the Marion Shovel operators, the people that knew how to run the big shovel. Another pretty hefty job class was running the big uke trucks down in that hauled the stuff. I was fortunate enough, after I was working down there for awhile, some of the guys on midnight shift taught me to operate the ukes, and then steelworkers earned 13 weeks' vacation because they'd been working there so long. As some of them went on vacation, I got to drive ukes, which was fantastic.

But getting back to how we got jobs. We sat there in this big room, and then we filled out and turned our papers in, and they'd go through our papers, and they'd have them in a stack, and they'd say, "Okay, here's your brass. Your brass is number 187. You were hired at 7:01 a.m. on such-and-such a date, on June 6, 1961. So-and-so, your brass number is 188. You were hired at at 7:02 a.m." Went through everybody, and the reason for assigning a specific time to everybody is, that established our seniority. If you had one minute seniority on somebody, well that was just your hiring order. So we were happy as pigs. They said, "Okay, so-and-so through so-and-so, you're going to be working for the rest of the day. So-and-so through so-and-so, you come in at 2:00 or 2:30 this afternoon and report here, and we'll take you to where you're going to be working. So-and-so and so-and-so, you come in at 10:30 tonight, and you're working midnight shift. So right away we got used to working different shifts.

I was fortunate; I was happy as a pig in swill, because I got to work at yards and docks. Yards and docks is where the labor pool was, that was down right next to the lake, so we got to work all over the plant. Some other people got assigned to the pelletizer, which was a nasty place to work, as far as I'm concerned, because it was so dirty. Others got assigned to the concentrator. Others got assigned to the crusher. So we were given jobs automatically, if you wanted to work there, it was a no-brainer. And then if you didn't screw up your first year out of high school, you could work there until you graduated from college. So for four years, you had a guaranteed job during the summer.

George Pope: It always strikes me how well our classmates turned out. Maybe Reserve hired smart and energetic people. But we had people from Beaver Bay and Finland who have also accomplished a lot in the professions and business. Maybe we had good teachers, although a lot of them were just five years older than we were. Maybe every class has many people who excel. Maybe it's the pioneer spirit. I don't know. We had a class of 56. I'll describe some of the class: Tony Auer became a professional actor, then became a Lutheran minister in a big church in California; JoAnne Backlund became a principal of a Twin Cities high school, got a PhD, and still works for the public education system; Jim Chupurdia became a director of business development for a major corporation; Julie Leines became a teacher and social activist; Joy Anne Manzer got a Ph.D. in mathematics and several other degrees; Nancy Metzinger became a nurse; Russell Moen became a postmaster; Roger Michalski played for the Gopher football team and got his master's in psychology, then became an executive for various corporations; Clair Nelson served in the Marines and eventually became a well-respected Lake County commissioner; Mike Sarff became a lieutenant colonel in the Army, got his M.S., and became a business executive; Marnie Tourje became a banker, moved to Paris, and then became a real estate professional in Santa Fe; I became a physician.

Pat Lorntson: We had four boys. All went to school and got a really good education. The oldest one has a doctorate in chemical engineering. The next oldest one retired from teaching math, senior high school math. Those were my two really orientated to something specific from the time they were quite young. Then my next two were the grease monkeys. One time the youngest one was home on a Saturday night. It was late in the evening, and he said, "I'm gonna go over to the garage and take the transmission out of my car." I thought, "If you were to tell me that you were going to do open heart surgery on the dog, I would feel this same way." I said to my husband, "Can he do that?" So yeah, he could do it. And he's got a big shop down in Elk River, and he's always done very well.

George Starkovich: Growing up in Silver Bay itself was a gift, I believe. When you look at our graduates now, the people that graduated 15, 20, 30 years ago are examples of what education in a small town can do. We have people who are internationally known as far as finance is concerned, as far as marine biology is concerned. We have people who are college professors. We have people who are lawyers that have argued cases before the highest courts in the land; we have physicians—renowned. One of my classmates is in charge of radiology at John Hopkins. Another person works for NASA. There's another one that works for the Atomic Energy Commission out of Los Alamos, New Mexico, in charge of monitoring all of the groundwater in the United States, in terms of half-lives of radioactive emissions that might be in the groundwater anywhere in the United States. Who would think that people from this little town of Silver Bay would spawn that kind of professionalism, and that kind of possibilities?

CHAPTER 6

MILEPOST 7

In the early 1970s, the federal and state governments lodged complaints against Reserve Mining Company for exceeding permit limits for the disposal of waste rock (tailings) in Lake Superior. A protracted federal court case ensued. At first, Judge Miles Lord oversaw the court proceedings. Many people viewed Lord as a highly biased environmental extremist with a generally anti-business and specifically anti-mining agenda. Silver Bay residents saw Lord wanting to take away their livelihoods. The hatred of Lord was palpable and pervasive. One piece of graffiti that existed for years inside the auditorium light booth at Kelley High School read, "[Expletive] Miles Lord"—a statement profound in its origin, coming from some teenager, whom one would not ordinarily expect to know anything about a federal court judge or court case. Attorneys for Reserve eventually moved to have Lord removed from the case, and the Court of Appeals did, in fact, remove him. Lord remained unapologetic, stating in an April 24, 1976, interview on Duluth's CBS TV affiliate, KDAL, "I concluded… that the stuff [emissions from Reserve's Silver Bay operations] is poisonous—deadly poison when inhaled in your lungs—that it is poisonous when inhaled and swallowed. You get an increase of cancer of the throat and of the esophagus, the stomach, the rectum—right down the line… Just because people haven't died yet—they aren't expected to die yet—it will take ten or 15 years. I don't want to be around this town then." During the thirty-five years after Lord made his statement on KDAL, his critics were vindicated by the actual community health record. Nevertheless, he had caused Silver Bay residents much mental anguish and economic hardship. After Lord was removed, the court case was resolved, with Reserve agreeing to build, at enormous expense, a disposal site inland from Silver Bay, at a location known as "Milepost 7." Consequently, events constituting the entire decade-long episode came to be known collectively by local residents as "Milepost 7" or "the Milepost 7 era."

Wayne Johnson: Problems started in 1970, and the federal government had made some complaints that the dumping into the lake was not approved and that [Reserve] had exceeded the Minnesota permit. So, I started working with the lawyers from Reserve, and I represented the city of Silver Bay, Beaver Bay, the town of Beaver Bay, the school districts, the Duluth Chamber of Commerce, and municipalities—all of those people had attorneys of their own. Because I had gotten involved right from the very beginning, they all asked that I be appointed as the liaison council for that group. So we represented 13 different groups, which we called the "northeastern Minnesota interveners" that intervened on the side of Reserve.

When I came down the first time to appear before Judge Lord, he called me into his chambers. Of course, he hated mining companies with a passion and let them know it, too. He called me into his chamber and said, "Wayne, why are you representing that bunch of bastards?" And I said, "Well, honestly the people I represent, they had lost their jobs, their livelihood, their entire careers." And he said, "Well I think you ought to switch over and go on the government side." I said, "Judge, I just can't do that," and he got up and he walked around his desk three or four times and sat down. He said, "Okay, I won't bother you anymore. You can represent whoever you want to represent," but he did run his courtroom very tough. He was not even polite to the corporate witnesses.

Matt Banovetz: The situation was very serious. Miles Lord shut the plant down once. I can remember Ed Furness calling me and saying, "Shut the plant down right now." So it was a possibility that the place could be closed down. Armco and Republic said that, if in fact they were harming and threatening the health of people, they would shut the plant down, but they didn't believe that was true. That was after a lot of consultants and researchers had done a lot of work. Then you had the threat of Miles Lord saying, "Shut that place down," which he did.

George Starkovich: I can remember some of the loneliest sounds that I ever heard—or not heard—was the car dump. The car dump is part of our living—that's what we hear. And when you don't hear the train, and you don't hear the car dump, something's wrong. It's part of what we grew up with. It's part of what we know. It's part of our lives. I believe that the PCA [Minnesota Pollution Control Agency] and the EPA [Environmental Protection Agency] caused a lot of mental anguish, a lot of physical pain. I believe that the stress that was brought on by a lot of the stuff that they did caused families to split up because of the economic crises that they caused and the unsureity that they caused. Some people were just throwing their keys on their table and leaving town. They were black days. If the conduct of the judicial officers was done in a respectful fashion, that's one thing, but that [darn] Miles Lord behaved like Judge Judy or some other comic on reality TV. It wouldn't be unusual for him to turn his back on people that were testifying on behalf of the company or giving evidence in regards to what was actually taking place. What is that? I mean, if a student in school would turn their back on a teacher, if the teacher's explaining something, they'd be called to task. Or if a teacher turned his back on a kid when the kid was asked a question and the teacher turned his back and pretended he wasn't listening!

Matt Banovetz: They had to fight in a court of appeals to get [the shutdown] overturned.

I was gone a lot, I flew all over the bloody country, either looking for money or trying to influence somebody, so I was gone a lot. My wife had a hard time understanding why I had to work so many hours, and I told her that there was just things that nobody else could approve but myself, and the people that were above me stayed home. They sent me to Washington or to Denver or to California or New York, things like that, but I felt that I owed it to the people that were working for Reserve to do my utmost to try to get the thing resolved.

When the trial first started, the mining company felt that [Miles Lord] was very fair and reasonable. What happened was, Reserve's lawyer told Miles Lord that there was a plan to get out of Lake Superior, and Miles Lord took it as gospel. About a week later, he wanted to know why they still weren't coming up with a plan to get out of Lake Superior. The lawyer never had authority from the mining company owner to say anything, because it wasn't approved, wasn't agreed upon by the two iron and steel companies. So, he had to go back and tell Miles Lord that there was no plan. That's when Miles Lord blew up. I felt sorry for a lot of hourly people. This was their whole life. They had worked for 20 years, a lot of them.

Pat Gordon: At the time we moved to Silver Bay, Reserve Mining Company was preparing for litigation with the environmental agencies and groups for dumping tailings into Lake Superior. During this time many of our jobs required extensive work to prepare Reserve's attorneys arguments. I remember copying employee records, as well as medical information for days on end. Everything was copied ten times, so there were numerous packing boxes sent to the respective litigation teams in Minneapolis. The argument was that people were being exposed to asbestos-like fibers (or carcinogens) from the tailings being dumped in Lake Superior. At the end of the litigation, all of these copied materials were shipped back to Silver Bay and stored in the basement of the Guest House.

Matt Banovetz: Every [darn] Friday, Judge Lord would say, "By Monday morning, I want this great big study done." We would work day and night, all weekend—you know—we had people from mining engineering or operations, whatever, we'd put out reams of paper, they'd plunk it down, and Judge Lord would throw it away. Next Friday he would give another one—that mean S.O.B. I can't believe that anybody could be as mean as he was, and he's no better today.

I heard him in Minneapolis. I joined the Rotary Club in Minneapolis, downtown. He was the main speaker, and that guy had the guts to say that people were dropping dead in the Silver Bay-Duluth area because of Reserve. I got on the phone in the next couple of days, and I called the Department of Health, and I told them what I was looking for. They said, "We suspected it." I called Dr. Leppink, in the County Health Office in Duluth—same story—nothing to it, and I knew it wasn't right, and that son-of-a-gun is still going around defending himself.

Marge Walentiny: My niece was marrying Miles Lord's son. We were at the wedding reception in Minneapolis for my niece, and of course Miles Lord was there for his side of the family. Someone pointed him out to us and said, "You want to talk to him?" And I said, "No, he's taken away our food. I'm not going to talk to him." My brother, he was a dentist, full of everything, you know? Miles Lord was walking by, and I was standing there… "Judge Lord, Judge Lord, I want you to meet someone." So he came over, and he said, "This is my sister, Marge Walentiny. She lives in Silver Bay." And he said, "Oh!" you know. Then he said, "How's your guts?" I said, "My guts is very well." I said, "We are very healthy up there." So then he said, "Does your husband work in the plant?" I said, "No, he works at the dispensary." He said, "Oh." He said, "Well don't tell him what I said." Well you know what I did. I told him what he said. Then you should see when we went to these hearings in Minneapolis.

Wayne Johnson: When we were going down to Saint Paul, to the federal courts, was probably the most distressing time and the most pessimistic time. But the people rallied, and we organized lots of people to go down and fill the courtroom and the lobby. I don't know if it impressed the judge, but it did tell the media that the public was concerned, not just the mining company.

Matt Banovetz: Wayne convinced a lot of the local politicians and the people that they had to stand up and be recognized. I think through his influence, if not direct activities on his part, he saw that a lot of local politicians and people showed up at hearings, and I think it had some influence, positive influence. Once, before the lawyers went before the court of appeals in St. Louis, Wayne made a speech to those judges that I thought was outstanding, and I thought that it was very influential in their decision. He's quite a guy. At one time, I never really appreciated this talent, but he did a great job. And I can see why some people haven't forgotten.

Tootie LeBlanc: How many trips down to the capital?

Ken Pellett: There was busload after busload that went down there.

Arlene Pellett: It was very traumatic, really. I mean, it wasn't a happy time.

Tootie LeBlanc: Together, we always stuck together like glue.

Lucy Malmo: I do remember that, as business people, we were involved. It was our livelihood. We had a 1970 Winnebago, and we'd go down to the hearings, and we loaded with people who wanted to go down, we'd drive down, and I don't know how many times we went with a load of people down to the hearings.

Marge Walentiny: This one woman [in the Twin Cities] said, "I'm getting sick and tired of this. I hope they're leaving now. They're nothing but a bunch of messy people." It was so funny because when people would go there, little kids were making lemonade from the town, and they were using our water. So as they were drinking it, I said, "You know that water you're drinking came from Silver Bay." When Anderson was there, the governor, and he came to talk, he said, "Gee, I better watch out so I don't get hit," and someone said, "People from Silver Bay are not that vicious." He'd have loved it if someone would've come and threw tomatoes at him.

Evie Buetow: We went down a couple times. They had buses going down.

Lois Hynes: Oh, I can remember a long line of cars one day. They started on Outer Drive, up at the hill, you know, and I just joined in. We went down, we went through Two Harbors, this whole big caravan.

Helen Robinson*: We used to get up at four o'clock in the morning to go on the bus to Minneapolis to meetings down there—the court hearings—so we could show people how we stood behind Reserve Mining. We had a caravan going to Duluth one time for a Democratic convention. I don't know how many miles of cars we had to show we stood behind Reserve Mining.

Clarence Roeben: We went down one time to testify at the hearing and sit in there, some of the boys from R&D. This was the proposal, when we were going to go to on land. Everybody knew we were going to be getting out of the lake. The company really agreed that we should put it in a confined area. Back in the days when taconite, or the natural ore was running out, the reason Silver Bay got built where it's built is because they could not get enough water for the process of this plant at the divide, or it would've been built at Babbitt.

So we testified down in the court there that particular day. Miles Lord got up and came over and shook my hand. That's how I got to meet Miles Lord, and of course we had the governor of Minnesota. We talked about strictly what we were going to do, and how we were going to do it, plus all the water samples and all the air samples that were taken. Each one of us talked for about 25-30 minutes, strictly on what we were going to be doing when we went to on land. Everybody agreed that we'd come out of the lake, but nothing was proven from the labs that we were doing what they said we were doing. We had data for that, so that ended it. Then they got into it, and finally Miles Lord turned, and he shut us up. And they appealed it in so many hours. Jerry Ketola said, "Clarence, tell your bosses that..." Hey, and Jim Reynolds wouldn't believe me. He said, "Where'd you get that information from?" He said, "They shut us down." I said, "In so many hours, we'll be reinstated. The appeals court will reinstate us. They can't keep us down, because there's nothing proven that we were doing what we were accused of doing." They settled it from there on, and it was very, very interesting. Lots of pressure. Those were trying times for Silver Bay. We had a lot of uncertainty. A lot of people had their time in, but lots had moved on and went elsewhere.

Bob Eckstrom: When they had the shutdown, somehow or another we were in Duluth camped overnight. The next day, they shut Silver Bay down when they had the big to-do in the arena or wherever it was.

Ruby Eckstrom: I think we walked down London Road. We had a march.

Bob Eckstrom: [U.S. Senator Hubert] Humphrey was there, and we waltzed him out of the arena in Duluth.

Bob Oslund: I was at that when Humphrey spoke. I think it was the DFL group down here—it was their annual convention or something. Humphrey said, "We do not need Reserve Mining Company." And everybody down here bought it, and everybody from Silver Bay drowned out those people down there when he made that statement. I don't know if he was running for office. This was when it was shut down. This was a big meeting in the arena, and everybody from town went down there. It was this huge delegation went down. We all sat up in the balcony, and Humphrey was talking to the DFL Party. It could've been '75 or '76, somewhere in there. There was this big clapping, and this big boo that came out from up above where all those people from Silver Bay were. It was very tumultuous.

Ruth Koepke: I was married to the mayor at that time. I think he got the best education that any mayor will ever get, because he went to Washington a few times, and we went to St. Paul many times—to Roseville—when they had the hearings on the plant. All the people from Chicago and Minneapolis were really against Reserve Mining, trying to shut it down. My daughter went to school in Mankato after she graduated from here, when the tailings discussion was, this kid was doing his paper on the tailings from Reserve Mining Company. I don't remember where he was from, but he was going to college in Mankato, and he said, "Them tailings are coming out of the lake, crossing Highway 61, and making it slippery." At the same time, the army worms were out, so when Linda went back to Mankato, we sent a bucket of tailings with her, and he said, "Oh, no that's not what that is." And she says, "Well I sort of happened to grow up there." He wouldn't believe that was what the tailings were. And I know that they always talk about 67 thousand tons of garbage—sewage—a day, and that's what all these big speakers from other areas were saying. "We can't allow this because all that sewage is going [into the lake]." And we tried to show them that this is waste rock, it's a natural thing.

Bob Oslund: The same time that was going on, that was when NSP [Northern States Power Company] was releasing radioactive waste from Monticello plant into the Minnesota River, or is it Mississippi River, that was going into the drinking water in St. Paul. That got the back page of the St. Paul paper at my parents, and the headline was Reserve.

Dave Prestidge: I had an auntie that lived in Illinois, and she said by the sound of things, it sounded like half to three-quarters of the lake was filled in. When she came up, she couldn't believe there was only such a little area that was really filled in with tailings.

Tim Bjella: A fellow that I thought would know those sort of things, he's the superintendent of schools in Central Minnesota, and he got on me one time because the mining company was dumping all this stuff in the lake, and I said, "It really doesn't amount to much, and it isn't going to make that much difference, except that we know that it'll show, you can see it." He says, "Yeah, but you're going to fill the lake up with this stuff." I said, "How much do you think they're putting in?" He said, "Well I saw this picture, and it showed Silver Bay, and then you've got this big pile of tailings." He says, "Pretty soon you're going to start filling…" I said, "Willy, it's 700 feet deep, just out there a ways. How long do you think it'll take?" Well, he says, "The picture said…" But I thought a guy that would know what was going on wouldn't be so stupid as to think that.

Bob Oslund: Jim Oxford is a biologist who lived a couple doors down from us. He raised trees for Mile Post 7, and he also raised rainbow trout in the delta and sent them to the state, and they said there was nothing wrong with them. They were raised in the delta and tailings, and the whole argument, remember, with Judge Lord, was that we were ingesting the fibers, not only breathing but ingesting. They found in those fish nothing, no evidence of anything that was going through their system.

Lloyd Houle: When going through all the hearings and stuff, I did the maintenance on the R&D building, and we dug a big hole in the back and filled it full of trout. They dumped the tailings right into that hole and then fish. You couldn't see nothing in there—it was gray—but you go throw a piece of sandwich out there, the fish would come up and grab it. Beautiful fish.

Wayne Johnson: On that water: The judge had some of the attorneys out in Reserve's boat, because he wanted to see what the water looked like. And they had some news people on the boat. And I had a glass that they'd been serving coffee or something, and I had this glass. I reached into the water and pulled up this cup of water, and of course the TV cameras were on me, and I drank the water down. The next day people were saying, "You could've poisoned yourself."

Jim Gordon: Many days were spent on Reserve's boat, *The Alma*, taking core samples of Lake Superior to determine the depth of the 'tailings' and how far they travelled down the shore of Lake Superior. There were many overnight trips on *The Alma*, and sometimes the weather was not the best to be on Lake Superior. At one time, the R&D crew took Judge Lord out on *The Alma* to see exactly what was going into the lake.

Wayne Johnson: Dan Rather said on his program [*CBS Evening News*] that people should roll up the windows when they were ten miles from Silver Bay and keep them rolled up until they went out of the area. The government had a doctor from Mount Sinai, Dr. Silakov, and he had made statement to the press that the water was not safe to drink. I don't recall exactly just what he said, but in essence he said it was poisoned, people should not drink it.

Mickey Lorntson: He claimed he wouldn't drive through Silver Bay with his windows open. He was supposed to be an expert on this stuff.

Chuck Kaiser: Right, right. He was the guy that said there'd be bodies in the streets, all that kind of stuff, in so many years. There's no question they were putting tailings in the lake, but it got screwed out of shape with all this misinformation. Honest-to-goodness facts, you can't dispute that, and that's what should've been, but there was too much speculation.

Karl Jevning*: Everything was so exaggerated. Like when they said the windows should be rolled up because the contamination was so bad. It was so silly.

Fran Jevning*: They played it for all it was worth and had people scared to death.

Wayne Johnson: We sent [Silakov] a report that night [after he made his press statement], he was supposed to testify the next day, and we had a report from the Minnesota Department of Health at the time saying that, even though the water was clouded, that it was safe to drink. We sent that over to his hotel room, probably about midnight or something like that. In the morning, he called me about 6:00 and said, "I don't know how they convinced me to say that. It was just a terrible thing to say." He said, "That's my philosophy, and I don't know I can correct it." I said, "Of course I can't advise you, but if I made a mistake, I would tell the judge what the facts were. The next day, he was the first witness called, and of course the judge was [leaning over and thinking], "This is going to be the killer." Ed Freeley asked the question, "Dr. Silakov, you said that water was poison. On what did you base that, that the people should not drink it?" And he said, "That was a terrible error on my part. I have no reason at all medically for saying there's anything wrong with that water." And Lord said, "You step down. Now." And that was the end of his testimony.

Tom Malmo: Weren't there some kids that said they couldn't go up to shore anymore because of the pollution in the air? They were being interviewed on TV.

Tim Bjella: We had a group of high school kids from St. Charles that came up to do a choir concert. As they came in the building, I'd made arrangement with their director for where they could be and what they could do, and I told them everything I thought they needed to know. When they came in the building, they all had their own bottle of water, because they wouldn't drink from our school fountain because it was "polluted."

Wayne Johnson: Judge Lord wanted to go up and see the proposed sites from the air, and at that time we talked about the Tettegouche site and of course Mile Post 7 and a couple of others. He had asked the state to furnish an airplane for him so he could fly around. Well, it so happens that the state didn't get the airplane up there, and he knew I had a plane, so he got ahold of me and said, "I want you to take me up and fly me around so I can get a good aerial view of all of those sites." One of his aides was with him, and so we got up, and we first flew down to that one that was at Two Harbors—Mile Post 20, I suppose. We flew around there, and he said, "That's fine." So then we flew around Mile Post 7, and I said, "You really want to get a good look at what this is from the swamp." He said, "No, looks pretty good from here. It shouldn't be destroyed." So I went down and just, tree tops, and he said, "I've seen enough." And then, "But I do want to see Tettegouche." And of course Tettegouche, as you know, is on a lot of hills with some little lakes, and I did the same thing. Down in the valley, I was a fighter pilot, so that's what I was doing.

Tim Bjella: If you had been at one of the hearings where Miles Lord was in charge, you could understand why people were so upset with him, because his point of view was obvious. He didn't care. He'd go in, his mind obviously [made up]. It made people very, very angry about his decisions, and I think rightly so.

Chuck Kaiser: He was definitely appointed because he was an environmentalist. That was his orientation. There was no attempt to put a judge in there that was going to be impartial. I don't know if there is such a thing, but this was way over the line. I think that's the way most people saw it—that it was a setup. There was no way you were going to win this thing. And, of course, if you look at the record, Miles Lord's decisions were overturned more than any other judge in the State of Minnesota, and that was because he did have that attitude, and then they put him in charge of this thing.

Ken Pellett: No matter how you want to look at it, this Judge Lord...

Pat LeBlanc: Was trying to pull the plant down.

Ken Pellett: And he did.

Tootie LeBlanc: He got the job done.

Ken Pellett: He accomplished what he set out to do. And he didn't always have the basic things to work with, but he had the power.

Ernest Bowman*: I don't hold a grudge, but Judge Lord—anybody that ignorant, you can't be mad at him, you have to feel sorry for him. He's a mental midget, as far as I'm concerned. They were pretty radical. The only thing that started that was they wanted Reserve out of the lake, and they didn't have a leg to stand on, so they brought up a false medical deal, and I mean it was just as false as counterfeit money: "Everybody is going to get asbestosis from drinking the water." Ain't a soul ever contracted anything like that in this town—nothing. That was a put up job.

Maggie King: It was a vendetta.

Chuck Kaiser: The people of Minnesota, and I think all over, were just incredibly ignorant of what this actually was. Two experiences illustrate this. One was, I went to a wedding down in St. Paul, and I forgot to bring along a sports coat, and so I had to go buy one. We were staying at, I think it was a Holiday Inn at that time. It was by the Sears building down there, right by the capitol. So I'm over there, and I got a sports coat. I was paying for it, and I used a credit card, and it was actually from the Duluth Sears store. And I gave it to this guy and he looked at it, and because of the number, he says, "Oh, you're from Duluth." And I says, "No, I'm not from Duluth, but I'm from Silver Bay." And he says, "Oh, stink city!" Well, you know, people had us confused with Cloquet and all kind of stuff. It's just one of those things where they didn't really know what was going on.

The other example: I went to a workshop at Mankato State one spring day, and this was back in the era when all the teachers were doing these innovative things, and they had a group there from the Cities, one of the suburbs. He had a bunch of students, and what they had was an environmental presentation. It was about Reserve Mining and their polluting of Lake Superior. So they got these slides, and they're showing these slides. And I was with a guy that was a teacher down in the suburbs. He and I knew each other just vaguely, but we were together that day, and he knew Lake Superior. He knew Silver Bay, so that was the difference between him and the rest of them. Anyhow, we're sitting there watching this thing, and he keeps looking at me and looking at me, because he knew I was going to say something. They had pictures of the water where the Beaver River was, and there was garbage and tires and all kinds of stuff floating around in there. And they had picture after picture of old cars sitting, rusted. And so when it was all done, they said, "Anybody got any questions?" And I go, "Where did you get those pictures?" I said, "They're dumping a kind of a talc into the water." I said, "They're not dumping old cars and tires in there. Where'd you get those pictures?" I says, "They aren't from Silver Bay. I live there. I know they're not from there." I said, "This guy next to me lives a part of the year up there. He knows it, too. So where'd you get those?" Well then they had to admit, they just went out and took pictures of whatever they could find of garbage in streams and stuff like that. I got up and walked out, and so did my friend. Before I walked out I said, "You just taught your kids to be terribly dishonest." I said, "I don't see that this has any value. I think the first thing I'd do is put it in the wastepaper basket and burn it and forget you ever did this." And we got up, and we walked out.

We ran into that all over all the time, even in the major news magazines. I remember one time there was a *Time* magazine that had one of those little maps they put in the corner of the story. And here's Duluth, and about a quarter of an inch away here's Silver Bay. You know, they had it, and then there was Two Harbors and all the way up, but they couldn't even place it geographically in the right place. Or Channel 10 in Duluth, ABC's affiliate down there. Every time they had a Silver Bay or a Reserve Mining story, they had a picture of Lax Lake with a Mile Post 7 posted on it. It was just dishonesty.

Pat Lorntson: Mickey was a commercial fisherman fishing herring for 50 years. He knows that lake like nobody else knows it. Tell them about the time you got so mad, I thought for sure he was going to lose his job when he came home and told me what he had done. [He] went down to the offices and talked to someone, I don't know who it was, and said, "You're an ostrich with your head in the sand if you think that there aren't tailings in the lake. My nets are full of it. The herring are not there because they don't go in dirty water." And I thought, "There goes the job."

Mickey Lorntson: I do remember speaking my mind a couple times. A lot of the company officials were quite ignorant about what was really going on. They just said it's not their problem, and they wouldn't look farther than that. And before they started that plant up, they had a model of the lake. They made a big model of the lake, and they poured this fine material in it, and of course it went right where they said it was gonna, and it did, it went to the bottom. But they didn't take into account all the current that's in the lake. The current was what carried that stuff to the surface. It only happened on certain occasions.

Maggie King: There were endless people who spoke of the chemicals that were being dumped into Lake Superior, and I don't know, hundreds of times, how I would say, "But it's rock. There's a bit of dust to the crushings and things."

Malvin Robinson*: I never figured it was as bad as they as they said. Crushing up granite rock and putting it in the lake wasn't hurting it that much. As far as I know, they never found any harm to anybody's body. They took us down, people that were here 20 years, to nonpartisan doctors in Duluth, and they never found any more rate of cancer here than anywhere else in the state. I don't know of anything they found out, even though they said it was bad all the time.

Ed Hynes: I think, in those years, with the court problems, I can say that the heart attack rate went up during that time. I served in the infantry in Korea. That wasn't as bad as it was here when our own government was trying to destroy us. I'm still mad about that. I think that was more politics than anything else. I could be wrong, but Miles Lord hated the mining industry. They didn't care what happened to the people up here. They just wanted to shut us down. It was a brutal time.

Lois Hynes: [One of the ladies] had ordered drapes at JC Penney's, and she went to pick them up, and they wouldn't accept a Silver Bay check. She said, "Well if you don't want my money, I don't want the drapes." They were custom-made, because they came and measured. She just walked out of the store.

Carol Roeben: Two Harbors wouldn't take your check. They would not take your check at Ben Franklin and at Ray's Shoes. Yep, because you worked for Reserve Mining. I've never had a bad check in my life, you know?

Ed Hynes: We used to go down to Brainerd with another couple for opening weekend, play some golf, until it got so we were defending ourselves all the time. We quit going. You know, we'd just get really defensive.

Lois Hynes: They just kept digging at you, "Well what's going on in Silver Bay now? How come" this and, you know.

Evelyn Turonie: I used to go to all of the golf things that they had in all of the towns, the invitationals, and I went to one in Duluth. I always seemed to play with this one lady. I don't remember how it came up, but she said something to me about, "Well you can't even use Lake Superior because you ruined it." I said, "I didn't even spit in it."

Ed Hynes: Someone said the teachers could tell if it was bad news, because the kids reacted. Our kids one time asked if we were going to be poor—if I was going to have a job. It's hard to forget it. I would write a letter or two to the newspaper during that period just to work off a good mad. Miles Lord once stated that the people in Silver Bay wouldn't have to go any further to find more work than he did, and the paper said he's just 15 miles from his work. Draw a 15-mile circle around Silver Bay, you got woods and water. It got unreal.

Helen Robinson*: I know the kids, when they were in high school, were concerned that we might have to move. We always said we would stay as long as the job was here. I know it did affect our own family and other ones at school, too.

Walter Skalsky*: You didn't know if you had a job or not. It was really rough. In fact, the whole town suffered. As far as Judge Lord was concerned, I don't think he went according to law, he went according to the way he felt. So, I don't know about these judges. They depend on their own feelings too much, or on what pressures they get.

Rose Elam: My husband was one of those that was in on the Judge Lord trial. Beech knew every pothole, every stream, every brook trout hole, and as he was giving his information, Judge Lord almost called him a liar, because he didn't think that anybody could know that much about the terrain, where to get that fish or where that stream was, where that little brook trout pond was.

George Starkovich: I remember when they had the hearings here. Frank Rukavina, because I was in charge of the theatre department at the time, asked me if I would take over the responsibility of making sure that the stage area was properly lit, properly mic'ed, yada yada yada, so they could conduct the hearings in there. I believe Mr. Lord even came up here. Judge Miles Lord is thought to be a savior, an environmental savior by many people in the State of Minnesota. To me, he's a black spot from the standpoint of, never at any time during that whole process did people take into account the effect that the actions of the EPA and the PCA [Environmental Protection Agency and Minnesota Pollution Control Agency] were having on the lives of the individuals in this community. It was like they were peripheral damage. We're going to go out, and we're going to get this company, this "corporate criminal," and we're going to hang them up to dry despite the cost.

Wayne Johnson: We got to a point where we moved to have [Miles Lord] removed as a judge, because he really put on the hat of an advocate rather than a jurist. The Court of Appeals agreed and removed him. The judge that was then appointed, Judge Edward Devitt, was a very, very scrupulous fellow and just hewed right to the line, no varying from any judicial misconduct. It was a long, long struggle—a lot of pessimism, a lot of people who lost their houses during the shutdown. To me, it was a time that was very, very stressful to so many people.

George Starkovich: The whole Mile Post 7 thing is just a, kind of a scary issue for me from the standpoint that they were not only dealing with the future of Reserve Mining Company, but they were dealing with the lives and health and well-being, mental and physical, of the people that lived in the community. Everything was fine, people were happy, people were productive, and things of that sort, and then all of a sudden you've got this black bird out of the south descending upon

Silver Bay in the form of the Environmental Protection Agency and the Pollution Control Agency.

Art Przybilla: I can remember a conversation we had at Davis's house, and he was saying that if he was to do it again, they wouldn't build the taconite plant on the lake. They would do it on the Range, like Erie did.

Ruth Koepke: But, you know, when they did this plant, they had two plans, and one was on land and one was lake. Well, it was going to be more feasible to dump in the lake. I have the book, and it has all the plans, and that's why they chose that, and there was no problem getting their permit through the state at that time.

George Starkovich: I think one of the biggest mistakes that Reserve ever made was that they did not leave a tree line between them, the dock facilities, and Highway 61. I think if they had the majority of the processing facilities up behind the hill and just had the shipping facilities south or east of Highway 61, the EPA thing and the PCA thing probably never would've happened. The PCA or the EPA said, "Okay, here's your standard. Your air must be as pure as the air that we sample in St. Paul." So they gave them those standards, alright? So at that time, St. Paul had a significant manufacturing economy—they had a significant industrial complex down there. Our people up here met those standards. A lot of the industry started to fold up and leave St. Paul, so when the industry leaves, what happens? The air changes, right? So now, because the air changed down in St. Paul, they tell us, "Hey, you're not meeting the standard anymore." "Well what do you mean we're not meeting the standard? We're meeting the standard that you gave us." "Oh, it says that you will meet the same standard as St. Paul. Here's what St. Paul has for air right now." "Well hey, you jerks, there's no manufacturing taking place in St. Paul." "That doesn't make any difference. This is what it says. It doesn't say 'based up on the manufacturing in St. Paul,' it's based on St. Paul air." You know, those are the kinds of games that PCA people played.

Charles Heinzen*: The State of Minnesota begged this plant to go when they started looking at it way back in the '40s. They did everything to the company to help them get going, and then a few years later, they wanted them to get out of the lake. I don't think they should have been in the lake in the first place, but being they were there, I think it was wrong to try and shut them down, which is what they were trying to do.

Maggie King: I remember 7/7/77.

Mickey Lorntson: Right, that number is just emblazoned. That was the date they had to get out of the lake. That was their cutoff.

Jim Andrews*: That was when the court had given Reserve that date to either agree to the Mile Post 7 thing or close down.

Wayne Johnson: I remember when the Minnesota Court of Appeals ruled that the three panel district judges were correct in their ruling that the company could go up to Mile Post 7, and I got a call from the clerk of the Supreme Court on a Sunday morning, and the court had just decided that they were affirming the district judges—because I knew the clerk and had worked pretty closely with him, he called me first. And I went to the various churches and made the announcement that day that the Supreme Court had affirmed the district court. And I think at that time Sychar met at 9:00, so I went there first. Then I went over to Faith and then to the U.P. and finally to St. Mary's. It kind of disrupted the religious service, because people all stood up and cheered.

George Starkovich: Finally settling on the fact they could build a tailing disposal out at Mile Post 7: That was a boon. It was a happy day to my recollection, feeling of rejoicing and stuff.

Pat LeBlanc: [The construction at Mile Post 7] was the biggest boom we ever had for fuel. We were out there, had trucks there 24 hours a day, seven days a week.

Tootie LeBlanc: We were living out in the country then, and in our garage, that was the repair shop for all the fuel trucks. And that was going 24 hours a day, one truck in, one truck out, drivers in. Coffee pot was on all the time, and they were coming and going, and oh boy.

Pat LeBlanc: It was a major project for us. I remember one time we were the second biggest lube contractor Mobil had in Minnesota, just because of Mile Post 7. We were bringing tankers out there two or three times a day, sometimes. It was big for us.

Tootie LeBlanc: We had a mechanic at the garage constantly fixing tires—all the rock they were driving over.

George Starkovich: Mile Post 7 brings up lots of negativity, because of the ravages of the PCA and the EPA. I think a lot of people's homes were ripped apart. We have seen the ravages of what happens to a mining company when it shuts down, when the people have to leave, when they've got no place to go, what it does to the kids, what it does to the families. And that's one of the worst things. We had a community that knew each other, that we could kind of lock arms together and stuff, and then the PCA and EPA came in and ripped us apart. That's how I look at it.

Ken Pellett: Mile Post 7 was a thing that caused a lot of heartaches for a lot of people. And when actually it was all boiled down, there wasn't a lot that really changed, other than the delta where the tailings still are, and of course they've upgraded it and put forest and a lot of timber on it now. But when you see what they're doing, and of course they have a lot of rules and regulations they have to follow. I mean, they have to keep X amount of water on top of everything. To me, now, it's a fantastic game refuge, is what it amounts to.

George Starkovich: When we finally got Mile Post 7, I thought it was a great day, because then again we saw the construction, but somehow the town was never the same after that. I think that took the financial stability away from Reserve Mining Company.

Matt Banovetz: I was convinced all the while, whether I had reason to believe, that it was going to work out some way. Unfortunately, the only way it got resolved was a tremendous expense of money on that project, Mile Post 7, and then a few engineering mistakes caused a lot more money to be spent. The first pipeline we put all the way up to the basin didn't work. It was rubber-lined pipe almost like what you'd call a hose, and the first time we tried it out, it acted like a snake. It was all over.

Jim Andrews*: I'm not positive what the economic situation was then in the steel industry, but I do know that the cost of the trial, the cost of the conversion to Mile Post 7 was enormous. Any corporation has just so much money, and when they run out of money, they're bankrupt. I would have liked not to have seen that terrible 7-7-77 date. That was a disaster. It went downhill from there.

CHAPTER 7

BANKRUPTCY

Burdened by the expense of building the Milepost 7 facility and by bad economic conditions in the steel industry in the early 1980s, Reserve Mining Company went bankrupt. This effectively ended Silver Bay's status as a "company town." Many residents were forced to move away to find employment elsewhere. Though another company eventually purchased the plant and restarted taconite processing operations, the character of the city was fundamentally changed.

Matt Banovetz*: I became the president of Reserve Mining Company—I think it was January 1981—and this was a very stressful time for Reserve Mining Company. We had just completed spending $371 million for the Milepost 7 project. It was difficult to get everything on line, operating the way we had anticipated. A lot of these problems still existed, but then, besides that, in 1982 began the first year of recession in the iron industry. And Reserve was a somewhat swing organization— what I mean by that is, Reserve Mining Company was controlled by only two steel companies. Most of the other companies had four or five partners, so it was very difficult for some of the other companies to agree on what the operating rate should be, but it was relatively simple for Republic Steel and Armco to agree to reduce operations at Reserve, so Reserve was hit harder than most other mining companies back in 1982 and 1983 regarding layoffs and cutbacks and temporary shutdowns. It was a very stressful time for employees and management during those times. I did fulfill the requirements for the president until 1986. Early in 1986, it was planned that the operation of Reserve Mining Company would be turned over to Pickands-Mather Company under a contract, and so Reserve would not be a free-standing company, as it had been since its conception. I had to make a decision whether I would stay on and work with the same responsibilities, for the most part, as general manager for Pickands-Mather Company or take my retirement, which I had earned. My first reaction was to stay with the transition and see it through, because I felt I would be able to help Reserve in this transition period and be able to do what I could in that job to protect the employees' benefits and such. However, personal problems became such that I changed my mind and decided that April 30, 1986, I would retire—take my early retirement—which I did.

Pat Lorntson: [Mickey had] his 30 years in December of '85. And then it went bankrupt in late spring, early summer. He was [among] the ones that had their 30 years and got their pensions. If you didn't make that 30 years, you didn't get it. I don't know at what point they did get it. I don't know how that ever came about, but the ones that actually had the 30 years in started right off with pensions. So we were lucky that way.

Bob Kind: I'll tell you, it was really tough around Silver Bay when Reserve Mining filed bankruptcy. That was tough.

Matt Banovetz*: I felt badly for all the people that got hurt. It was so sad. I never dreamed anything like that would happen. I really thought that it would be a successful operation. It most likely would have been, and very successful, had it not been for LTV's bankruptcy and then everything tumbled, and it was very sad. I spent a lot of sleepless nights thinking about the people who got hurt badly—good people, good operation.

Clarence Roeben: We had a lot of people move away from us here after the doors closed.

Lloyd Houle: The county used to have 13,450 people. When Reserve closed, it went down to 10,000.

Carol Roeben: And it was a lot of the younger ones, people with children.

Wayne Johnson: The population [of Silver Bay] went from about 3,200 down to about 1,400 in a very short time.

Judy Kaiser: At that time, I was at the credit union, and we had our parking lot at filled with items that had been repossessed. It was hard times.

Pat Lorntson: I taught from '65 until '85. I taught first grade, and in those last five years, I just saw the parents' support declined, and they would come in for conferences and say, "Okay, I don't care if he can't read, but how's his math?" And then one parent said, "If that teacher thinks I'm going to stay home at night to help because my kids have to do homework, they're crazy." And I thought, something has happened with the parents, with all these parents. The last few years, I didn't know if I was going to be able to stay there. It just went downhill.

Maggie King: It was a very depressing time.

Chuck Kaiser: You'd come into a classroom, and everybody just sat there, and it was tough.

Maggie King: I had understood that the four years after '86, the yearbooks were dedicated to their classmates who were gone, and that, emotionally, it was quite a sociological downer for these kids.

Chuck Kaiser: My youngest, Ward, was in one of the tiniest classes. And I remember those kids stood in that cafeteria down there after graduating, and—I don't care, boys, girls, toughest, biggest ones—they all just cried. And it was all because of the fact that most of their classmates had left. I mean, we had valedictorians, salutatorians scattered all over the state of Minnesota. You know, some of our best kids were the ones. Our best kids left, along with a lot of others. They went to other schools, and they were top-notch students there. And these were all friends of the ones that stayed. They just cried. I mean, it was the saddest thing I can remember. I went to every graduation.

Maggie King: They had struggled and struggled to keep a stiff upper lip through all of that duress.

Lucy Malmo: When things changed [at the clinic, because the company went under], people thought, "Well what's the matter? How come…." They were so used to being able to go there day and night, and I was always disappointed. Dr. Clifford had been there for a long time, and he needed help. Everything had been supplied, the supplies all came from Reserve, and here was a clinic with no income, and the people didn't group together and get behind him to purchase and run the clinic. They always thought, well it was always easy come; they didn't have to worry about expenses for things. Reserve was the big daddy to everybody for everything that. We always said this was a different community than a regular town because the company provided so many things for everyone.

Ken Pellett: When Reserve Mining Company went down into bankruptcy, there was a lot of homes in this town you could buy it for a song. The house right across the street from us sold for $6,000. It was a lot of semi-retired people came here, bought homes for recreation purposes, there was some of them showed up only summertime and fishing season and for snowmobiles, and they hunt. And then we got the different clientele of people came to town because they were cheap houses. Not all good, but that's the way the world is. We have to learn to live with some of these people.

Tootie LeBlanc: Well they never really added to the town, I mean, as far as stability at all.

Arlene Pellett: And I think, too, it changed in a way, because then you didn't know your neighbor two doors down, maybe, where before you knew everybody on your street. That had changed then, and it had a different atmosphere, because some of those people came maybe on weekends or in the summer. They'd snowmobile on the weekends in winter, so they didn't really live there all the time.

Clarence Roeben: I'm happy for those snowbirds that bought homes, acquired those homes and help us. And they keep the town up, too. It costs lots of money to maintain our police force, our streets.

Karl Jevning*: It is a different group of people in town now. Before, if you didn't work for Reserve or in the stores or businesses in town, you didn't live in Silver Bay. We didn't have any retirees living here back in the '50s and '60s. Now, I suppose one-third of us are retired.

Helen Robinson*: There's not so many little kids on the street. There used to be 30 or 40 kids on Ives Road, and now there's not that many. There's not as many younger couples; we're all getting older and grandparents now instead of younger and raising our children.

Malvin Robinson*: You used to know everybody in every house in town, and now you don't know half or a quarter of them.

Clarence Roeben: Oh 1986, July 18, I was right there. I helped put the locks on the next day. That was very devastating. I got appointed by the bankruptcy judge in New York, and we shut this place, finished it up. They sent us special locks, and we locked it up. And then I was asked to help periodically during the bankruptcy and find different files, and they had people here, and they set up, and we went from one client [to another]—people that they owed money, those people they were doing business with one at a time. You didn't deal with the whole group at one time, just one at a time. It's very devastating to sit in those areas; you had to be there just for a witness. I had nothing to do with speaking or anything but helped gather the information that they needed. Everybody should have that opportunity to close it up and then work during the bankruptcy. Those faces from those vendors—they never forget you, because a face means more than a name.

It was hard when we went back to work to start up. We worked hard. They had a good bunch of management boys here that helped, that worked together and was right there. My duties were to go in every department and work with maintenance as well as operating people. The reason at the tail end I got my hands wet during Reserve days was maintenance, at the very end before we went down completely. 1986, the 18th day of July. Never forget it.

They had meetings in St. Paul, and Cyprus Minerals agreed that they would open this as fast as they could, and that was in July. It was almost three years to the day when we got the word, and they started regrouping and put us back. Cleveland Cliffs outbid Cyprus Minerals, because they were willing to pay four or five million dollars more, plus the inventory that was in stores. Our governor at the time was Rudy Perpich, and he said, "I want it open now. I want people back to work." That's how Cyprus Minerals said that they would start it immediately, if they got the opportunity.

There was lots of trying times. I mean, one trip to Pennsylvania—to Harrisburg—where we had all the bolts and metals made during Reserve days, and go there and meet with them and deal with the ware parts that it took to run the crushers, bolts, and metals, both Babbitt and here, and we get 30 days' credit. And after we got done discussing there, I had to buy that; it was thrown right at me. They were impressed that they could get 30 days, and one of the board members out there said, "We'll give you 60 days, provided we get our money in 60 days." They were ones that they owed several million dollars when she went down. I was amazed. Pretty soon they said, "You can have 120 days." And Dave DeLeo was our first CEO under Cyprus Minerals, and he wanted to know what I did to get 120 days. I hand-delivered that to the head of accounts payable, and saw that check got mailed before the 120 days. It was a lot of trying times with that. And of course I can't blame a lot of creditors. I mean, you get burnt once, it's tough, it's the hardest job to be involved, and I never dreamt that I'd ever be involved again in startup like that. But I enjoyed it, meeting the people and so forth. They were nice people up there in Harrisburg—very, very good. The people up in Hibbing, the rigging and wiring, they're good people. They've got good people in Duluth, and they're in the business, like Industrial Welders.

George Starkovich: When Reserve Mining Company closed down: bad times, bad news. Didn't know what the heck was going to happen.

Lloyd Houle: I retired two years before the plant went down. I was a pretty good friend of [Governor] Rudy Perpich's, so he kept me involved when he'd go out to the director's meeting. He called up one day, and he said, "I want to get this Reserve thing settled." One time when we were having dinner on Sunday, Rudy called up and he said, "You know, we're going to get that plant open," and I said, "Well, that sounds good." When he went down and announced the opening of the vets' home at Campton, he got a call that said, "Cyprus is moving in." Those were some tough days there between '84 and '86.

George Starkovich: And then Cyprus came in. You can print this in big bold letters. I was invited to a meeting to hear the Cyprus presentation, and I was aghast when these people were talking. They said, "Yada yada yada, we want to welcome you to this briefing," or whatever. "We're going to talk to you a little bit about our operation here in Silver Bay. We are Cyprus. We are here to produce taconite pellets. *We are not here to form a partnership with the community.* We are not here to maintain the golf course. We are not here to furnish the school district or the city with anything. We are not dut dut dut dut da. We are not dut dut dut dut da. We are a mining company, and that's what we are here to do." I was going, "You've gotta be kidding me. What is this?" Cyprus Mining, as far as I'm concerned, is a black hole. I think what they did, they came in here to take the best of what was left and to rip the guts out of it.

So then when Cleveland Cliffs came in, and Northshore Mining came in, they wanted a non-union shop, and our people were kind of wary of working in a non-union shop, but the people that worked for Cliffs now are very, very happy. They have profit-sharing, they have bonuses. People that want to work an honest day's time for an honest wage have no problem. It's a very lucrative place to work, from my understanding. I understand they're very well paid. Their good workers are rewarded. Those that don't work well and don't fit into the system are dismissed. They don't have any tolerance for people that use drugs or come to work drunk or things of that sort. Again, this is stuff that I've been told. I have a great respect for Cliffs, and Cliffs has reinstated some things that we lost as a result of Reserve Mining Company going under. Reserve Mining Company for years gave a sizable scholarship to a male recipient and a female recipient. When they sold it, that particular scholarship was no long available. But Cliffs has now set up another scholarship program [for which dependents of Cliffs employees are eligible].

Clarence Roeben: Oh, company town. Well, I will say Silver Bay was a good town to raise a family in. The mining company treated us very, very well as far as our education was, because they had something to offer for our young people here.

So Reserve days, Silver Bay was very, very good, and everybody looked out for everybody. I mean, you looked out for your neighbor, and I think that's the key. You don't have that as much today as you did back then. We've got people right next to us that are renting. I've met them once, I don't remember their last name, and they're next door. Back in the days of Reserve, the kids got acquainted with the neighbor kids, and the people two blocks down, and we were more united as a group than we are today. And that's what I see.

Index *(Interviewees in italics)*

90